"

The ultimate 'how to' guide for the corpo[...]
the champion of all those hard-working people trying to make
innovation work at scale.

Sir Charles Allen, CBE

In an inspirational and practical book, Matt explores the 'logic
of magic' at work and gives us new tricks to make it happen.
Read only if you are ready to behave accordingly!

Marc Mathieu, Senior Vice President, Unilever

At Zappos, our belief is that if we get the culture right, most of
the other stuff, like delivering great customer service or building
a long term enduring brand, will happen naturally on its own.
This book lifts the lid on much of the hard work needed to create
buzzing, innovative and adventurous companies.

Tony Hsieh, *NY Times* best-selling author of *Delivering Happiness*
and CEO of Zappos.com, Inc.

One of the rare business books that you will actually read from
start to finish.

Julian Birkinshaw, Professor of Strategy and Entrepreneurship,
London Business School

Matt Kingdon has woven twenty years of front-line innovation
experience into a compelling offering for the many heroic
innovators working against the odds in established
organisations. Bottom line: you are not alone and this is the
practical guide for you.

John Kao, founder of the Institute for Large Scale Innovation,
creator of Harvard Business School's innovation program,
Chair of the World Economic Forum's Global Advisory Council on
Innovation, author of *Jamming*, and Frank Zappa's keyboard player

"

The Science of Serendipity

How to Unlock the Promise of Innovation in Large Organisations

Matt Kingdon

WILEY

A John Wiley and Sons, Ltd, Publication

This edition first published in 2012 by John Wiley & Sons Ltd
© 2012 ?What If! Limited

Main photography by Jake Hilder of Jake Hilder Photography
www.jakehilderphotography.co.uk

Registered office
John Wiley & Sons Ltd, The Atrium, Southern Gate, Chichester, West Sussex, PO19 8SQ,
United Kingdom

For details of our global editorial offices, for customer services and for information about how
to apply for permission to reuse the copyright material in this book please see our website at
www.wiley.com.

Wiley publishes in a variety of print and electronic formats and by print-on-demand. Some
material included with standard print versions of this book may not be included in e-books or
in print-on-demand. If this book refers to media such as a CD or DVD that is not incl uded
in the version you purchased, you may download this material at http://booksupport.wiley.
com. For more information about Wiley products, visit www.wiley.com.

Designations used by companies to distinguish their products are often claimed as trademarks.
All brand names and product names used in this book are trade names, service marks,
trademarks or registered trademarks of their respective owners. The publisher is not associated
with any product or vendor mentioned in this book. This publication is designed to provide
accurate and authoritative information in regard to the subject matter covered. It is sold
on the understanding that the publisher is not engaged in rendering professional services.
If professional advice or other expert assistance is required, the services of a competent
professional should be sought.

Library of Congress Cataloging-in-Publication Data
ISBN 978-1-118-47810-3

A catalogue record for this book is available from the British Library.
ISBN 978-1-118-47810-3 (paperback) ISBN 978-1-118-47811-0 (ebk)
ISBN 978-1-118-47812-7 (ebk) ISBN 978-1-118-47813-4 (ebk)

Set in 10.5/16pt ITC Mendoza Roman by Sparks – www.sparkspublishing.com
Text design by ?What If! Limited
Printed in Italy by Printer Trento

This book is dedicated to my great friend,
business partner and co-enthusiast of 20 years in
this crazy business – Dave Allan

Contents

Introduction

The Real Heroes of Innovation

W hat could be more exciting than starting with a blank sheet of paper and creating something of real value? Making something out of nothing, pointing to something that's in the marketplace and saying *'I did that'*.

In life, there isn't much that's more exciting than this.

Being in the right place at the right time, seeing what no one else has seen, connecting the dots and having the perseverance to drive an idea all the way to launch and commercial success. This is the entrepreneur story that we know well.

But somehow this story has been stolen by the start-up. The word 'entrepreneur' or even 'innovation' has become synonymous with supercool, hyperintelligent and astonishingly young guys making millions.

I want to explore something that's equally as challenging as the start-up story and – if you get it right – highly rewarding. I want to explore the story of innovation in large organisations where the need to refresh is ever-present. All companies were start-ups once and for many of them that spirit lies dormant, waiting to be reactivated.

This book gets under the skin of how you can make innovation really happen in organisations that have an embedded operational mindset. In my experience these are generally large organisations. I hope you find it a practical book, rich in the stories and lessons learned from the frontline of corporate innovation.

Established companies have their own rhythm and new suggestions are often met with crossed arms. These companies know they need to take a few risks and try doing things differently. But it's tough, really tough. There seem to be roadblocks everywhere. The organisation is almost hardwired to repeat success and reduce risk, and now it is being asked to do the opposite. Somehow the battle to innovate is being fought at work and not in the marketplace.

Every few years at ?What If! we take the innovative temperature of our clients. In 2012 we asked 50 senior executives responsible for innovation in large global companies to tell us how the innovation 'landscape' was changing. They told us that the future feels much more uncertain, that it has become extremely difficult to plan for innovation and that executives need to be better equipped to deal with ambiguity. They reported that the need for disruption is forcing people to look beyond their category and comfort zone and that stakeholder relationships are getting more complex, with more hurdles to overcome than ever before.

It's in places like these that the real heroes of business work. To innovate at scale and create wealth and employment for many is in my view the most noble of commercial challenges. I want to tell the stories of the people who do this, how they have struggled, how they have succeeded and what this can teach us.

I want all those executives who've had their entrepreneurial mojo beaten out of them – or who think it's the preserve of the groovy – to think again. After 20 years of innovating with large companies I know that serendipitous invention and the creative exploitation of ideas is a muscle that you can choose to work out or allow to wither.

> **"**
>
> *Serendipitous invention and the creative exploitation of ideas is a muscle that you can choose to work out or allow to wither*

Serendipity – or seemingly 'happy accidents' – is a fascinating concept and I'll define it in detail in just a few pages. The concepts of serendipity and innovation are sibling and they somewhat merge in this book. Serendipity is the connective raw material for successful innovation. It's an important element of innovation, especially in a large company where many have their heads down and their peripheral vision reduced. Innovation is the commercialising of what looks to the outsider like a 'lucky break'. You can't deliver innovation in a large organisation unless you have a practical grip on what serendipity really is and how you can make it work for you.

In calling this the book *The Science of Serendipity* I'm using the term 'science' with considerable licence. Over five chapters I've bundled a series of observations about how people prepare themselves so that they can connect the seemingly unconnected and push on to make something out of these connections in their organisation. Without doubt there are practical steps you can take to be 'lucky' and hit upon the next big thing. Together these five chapters form a logic or a 'science' to the serendipitous discovery and exploitation of ideas. This book isn't about theory; it's a practical book based on practical experience for those grappling with innovation at scale.

Fundamentally, innovation is about how human beings get inspired to look in new places, work together and react to the unwelcome and the unexpected. Creating innovation within a large organisation takes a mix of determination, provocation, experimentation and political savvy. I've included here many stories, observations and lessons learnt from a wide variety of sectors. Hopefully you'll agree with me that it's both fascinating and instructive to explore beyond the boundaries of your industry and take a peek at how others are innovating.

From Big to Small to Big

I love telling stories, particularly innovation stories. I love the drama and the essential 'human-ness' of these stories. I take innovation seriously but not solemnly; as a subject it deserves to be provocative, playful and engaging.

My own story is of working for a big company, then a small company that now works with big companies. I started work in the 1980s as a marketer with Unilever, the giant consumer goods company. I spent years figuring out how to help people all over the world get cleaner clothes, enjoy fragrant armpits, have shinier kitchens and remove unimaginably awful stains from their loos. It was an inspiring education in how a large company connects with its customers and makes them happy.

Then in 1992, when I was 29, I had one of those Maslow Moments when you realise what all that self-actualisation stuff is really about. I teamed up with a colleague – Dave Allan. We had no money, no partners, no kids, no debts – we actually had nothing apart from a crazy desire to reinvent the way large businesses develop new stuff. So we decided to set up a company called ?What If! in London. What we lacked in a plan we made up for in optimism.

Today, nearly 20 years later, we have 250 colleagues (we call them '?What If!ers') and offices in three continents. Over the past two decades we have worked with hundreds of great businesses helping them to ignite and sustain a radically more innovative approach to business. We've partnered with some of the world's most ambitious companies in most market sectors – all of them looking to accelerate growth through innovation. We have completed over 5000 innovation engagements in 45 countries and coached over 50,000 people to help strengthen their innovation muscles.

But when we started we weren't that great. Looking back I shudder to think how naive we were. Our first innovation assignment did not light up our client. It was clear that we hadn't spent enough time with consumers in their own homes, we hadn't developed the commercial argument behind our ideas and we hadn't understood what was driving the people within our client's organisation who had to say 'yes' to the idea. Feeling down – in a dive of a bar in north London – Dave and I scribbled down how we were going to react to what felt like a disaster. We didn't know it then but we were committing ourselves to the core innovation principles that would evolve to become the foundation of our business. Pity I don't still have that scrap of paper; but here's what we agreed:

- Creativity alone is futile. A successful commercial launch of an idea is all that matters.

- Understanding how customers live their whole lives, not just how they react to a particular category is critical.

- We'll always make ideas real and try hard not to slip into a client's business jargon.

- Every assignment we work on we'll try some new way to get inspiration.

- Finally, innovation is all about our behaviour – how we react to each other's ideas, how we create an expectation that we'll 'lean in' to an idea and how we'll be tough with each other when we think the other's idea stinks.

These principles have remained pretty true over 20 years. Along the way we've gathered an amazing team that has helped us to evolve our approach, engagement after engagement, year after year.

There's one thing I've always believed is critical in growing a business – paranoia. Seriously, I think it's a good thing. I've always been criticised for being upset with the things around me; I don't care. I think it's good to look over your shoulder every day; I like to worry all the time. I like restless people – always trying new stuff, never satisfied with things.

So at ?What If! we've tried just about every innovation tool, structure, behaviour, philosophy – call them what you will – we've tried them. Twenty years ago we started recruiting supertalkative multilingual consumers, arranged them into panels and trained them to be creative. We developed a homegrown philosophy that involved literally moving in and living with customers. We started recruiting what we called 'naive experts' – people with tangential but surprisingly useful expertise to our clients. We banned the use of our clients' internal business jargon and forced ourselves to talk only in the language their consumers would use. We pioneered meetings with clients on buses, in bedrooms, in kitchens – anywhere to better the connection with 'reality'.

By the mid 1990s we had established a 'Realness' team whose job was to translate ideas into physical objects, on the spot. We never called any of this 'ethnography' or 'prototyping' or 'customer centricity'; to us it was just one huge rolling experiment to find the best way to innovate. In 1996 we started training our clients in the techniques of innovation and flexible thinking. Many of our innovation principles are embedded into the training and development programmes of the world's most successful companies.

Ten years ago we started to realise just how exciting the world of innovation was becoming. Although it was useful to read about companies doing great stuff, it had far more impact to visit them and hear from the top brass themselves about how innovation really works. We established our 'TopDog' study tours and today have taken over 400 senior executives on intensive immersion experiences. We've visited over 50 organisations ranked as the world's leading innovators. We've seen companies up close and personal such as Google, Apple, WL Gore, Walmart, Lego, IKEA and many more. After each tour we've worked with the 20 or so executives in attendance to distil the learning. We've literally been all over the world in our pursuit of innovation excellence.

One of the things we insist on during our visits is that the company leaders talk informally and from the heart about their struggle to innovate. We encourage them to go backstage to the warehouse, the staff canteen or the loading bay and then we'll quiz staff to see if what we're hearing stacks up. These visits, and the debates they have provoked, have surfaced fascinating nuances in how innovation really happens.

More recently, as our clients have become more ambitious around innovation, our work has expanded to the scale of organisational transformation. How can a large organisation start to work with agility and how can it do this day after day? Our years spent at the coalface of innovation have given our approach to agenda setting at the leadership level, to educational programmes and to innovation projects, a uniquely practical perspective.

About Serendipity

Serendipity is an intriguing word. Alongside 'Irish Eyes' and 'Island Time' it's in the top ten of boat names in the US. The word 'serendipity' has an undeniably mellifluous quality about it. You can roll it enjoyably around your tongue and it regularly tops the charts of favourite English words, alongside discombobulate, twiffler and mumpsimus.

These are enjoyable facts but they don't help us get under the skin of serendipity or understand how it can unlock all that innovation promises.

To understand the concept of serendipity we have to go back a thousand years to a story emanating from the East and retold many times over the centuries.

The tale is charming. Three Princes of Serendip (today we know this as Sri Lanka) were sent by their father, the king, on a journey to test their suitability to reign. Along the way they met a camel driver who asked them about his lost camel. The three princes were able to describe the camel in much detail: 'Your lost camel is blind in one eye, is missing a tooth and is carrying butter and honey'. So accurate was the description that suspicions were raised and the princes thrown into jail. But later they were pardoned as it became clear that they had merely connected many separate observations together to produce the uncannily accurate story.

On their travels the princes had seen grass eaten from one side of the verge and reckoned an animal blind in one eye must have caused this. Grass was scattered unevenly, so a tooth must have been missing. And the ants on one side of the road indicated the presence of butter, the flies on the other side of the road honey. The story continues along a similar vein, each twist sees the clever princes combine seemingly casual observations – things that most people might miss – into something more meaningful.

> *'This discovery, indeed, is almost of that kind which I call Serendipity, a very expressive word'*

This fairy tale was popular in the bustling metropolis of Venice in the sixteenth century. I can imagine it as a sort of early day detective story; its clever twists and reasoning appreciated during the Renaissance. In the English language the word serendipity surfaced relatively recently – 250 years ago. The earliest known usage is by Horace Walpole, son of a Prime Minister and man of letters. In 1754 he mentions the Three Princes of Serendip who 'were always making discoveries, by accidents and sagacity, of things they were not in quest of' and 'This discovery, indeed, is almost of that kind which I call Serendipity, a very expressive word.'

Most dictionaries define serendipity as the occurrence of events by chance in a happy or beneficial way – a 'happy accident'. This definition seems to imply serendipity is purely a chance or a random kind of thing. The 'sagacity' element Walpole mentions seems to have been dropped.

The definition of serendipity that I'm using assumes a happy and profitable outcome that may be unanticipated but has not been found purely by chance. What looks like luck – a 'happy accident' – is in reality hard-earned.

> **"**
>
> *What looks like luck – a 'happy accident' – is in reality hard-earned*

This concept seems to be wholly suited to the reality of what it feels like to innovate. So many successful innovation stories involve hard-working people who set out on a mission. Their precise goal may be a little fuzzy, but they are determined to right some wrongs and, as Steve Jobs said, put a 'dent in the universe'. These people have cast their nets wide. Maybe they have broad experience or maybe they have a diverse team working for them. The more they get out and about and fill their mental filing cabinet with provocative stimulus, the more likely they are to spot patterns and make some interesting connections. This works the intuition muscle; pretty soon they get confident with their gut. Louis Pasteur was aware of this when he commented 'chance favours only the prepared mind'.

Listen to innovators describe how they felt along their journey. Only they know how hard they worked to make a single new connection and how many connections failed to yield anything of value. Only they know how well they prepared their people, so that when an opportunity appeared they spotted it immediately and made it into something. Luck for them doesn't exist – it's a romantic, illusory concept. They have made their own success. 'Luck' is the label of the onlooker.

Serendipity is more than just setting yourself up so that great connections become more likely; it delivers a result as well. You can't be serendipitous or innovative if you don't know how to deal, there and then, with the connection you've just made. Think of it as a game of two halves. First we collide with as much stimulus as possible; next we seize on a connection and do something about it. This is why serendipity fits so well with innovation and not creativity. To stumble upon a new connection may be what some label 'creative', but to commercialise it is an altogether different game. This is innovation and that's the game we're interested in.

'The harder I practice, the luckier I get.'

Variously attributed

Getting lucky

It's August 1993 and 12 male volunteers are reporting back the effects of a potential new angina drug to a Pfizer clinical research associate in Cardiff, Wales. One of the men reports an unusual finding: sustained and frequent erections. After he'd broken the ice, all the others chorused agreement.

Nonplussed, the clinician explains the unexpected finding to the scientist leading the trials, Dr David Brown, a senior Pfizer research chemist. But when she does, Brown sits bolt upright. Brown knew he was, so to speak, on to something big. But he had no idea that he'd discovered what was to become Viagra, a $30bn blockbuster.

After some persuasion, Brown got an extension to continue the trials – at Southmead Hospital in Bristol where they had a specialist erectile dysfunction unit. This time the trialists were fitted with a device called a 'Rigiscan' (please use your imagination here) and asked to watch pornographic movies. Then they were allowed to take the pills home to see how well they worked under more normal conditions.

A week later, when they returned to report their results, something unexpected happened. Several of the men refused to give the pills back claiming it had radically improved their sex lives. 'It was very humbling and gratifying to see how much happier these men were', says Brown. 'They reported they had a normal sex life with their wives for the first time in years.'

Eventually the men were persuaded to return the pills on the condition that the next time there was a clinical trial they would be amongst the first asked to take part. This was a promise that Brown and his team were able to fulfil several months later. Brown adds: 'The project went from nearly dead to top priority globally, a full development programme.' So great were expectations that when Viagra was eventually launched in 1998, Pfizer's share price had doubled. Over the next few years Pfizer went on to become the world's largest pharmaceutical company and also, for a time, the world's most valuable company by market capitalisation.

We need to dig a little deeper to understand the serendipitous nature of this story. A confluence of events contributed to Brown's ability to spot the potential of the angina drug.

First: several years earlier Brown had tried but failed to get Pfizer's backing to start a research project to help men suffering from erectile dysfunction (ED). The only science known at the time led him to suggest a drug that acted directly on the brain and promoted sexual arousal. As Brown says: 'This was just too dangerous as a concept and quite rightly I didn't get the green light.' Although he was leading an angina project, Brown was aware of the commercial opportunity in ED and critically that an ED drug couldn't act centrally, in other words, on the brain.

Second: his offices and labs were, in his words '... old and dilapidated. We were crammed into a quite small space with the whole team of chemists and biologists bumping into each other all the time, which fortunately led to constant exchange of information, ideas and views without the need for formal meetings ... somehow that building coincided with a time of Pfizer's greatest innovations.' Inevitably, it was in a corridor conversation that Brown learnt about a new scientific discovery of the biochemical role of a gas called nitric oxide. Until then no one had suspected its ability to dilate the blood vessel in the corpus cavernosum – the blood vessel in the penis that opens up during an erection.

Viagra, as it became known, potentiated the action of nitric oxide. This meant that Brown and his colleagues Nicholas Terrett and Andy Bell were able to put two and two together when they heard about the unexpected side effects. A couple of years earlier and he just wouldn't have understood the link between the pharmacology and the men's lusty claims.

From his earlier ED proposal, he also knew Pfizer would support a peripherally acting but not a centrally acting drug. In other words you had to feel horny for the science to work, not have the science make you feel horny. When the results came through from Cardiff, Brown not only knew why the drug was initiating erections, he thought that Pfizer would support it.

Brown, who is named as the co-inventor of Viagra on the Pfizer patent, was also instrumental in the development of two other successful Pfizer drugs and, a few years later, became Global Head of Drug Discovery at Hoffman La-Roche in Switzerland leading the efforts of 2000 research scientists. Today he chairs several start-up biotech companies in Cambridge, England, and remembers the days of the old office in Kent with fondness: 'They were the most uncomfortable and yet the most productive.'

The story of the serendipitous discovery of Viagra is packed with learning for innovators. If Brown hadn't been rejected in his early attempts to work on ED, if Brown hadn't worked out of a crush of an office – if these things hadn't have happened then maybe Pfizer would never have discovered its winning product. But Brown and Pfizer weren't just lucky. Because he was prepared, then chance did favour him.

So, determination, a diverse but intimate network, intuition and agility – these are all concepts found in the 1000-year-old tale of the Three Princes of Serendip and the modern-day invention of Viagra. These are the ingredients of innovation. They seem to make for an altogether more realistic innovation recipe than one that claims innovation is somehow preordained through great strategic thought and rigorous planning.

Don't Think Too Hard, Don't Talk Too Much, Just Try It

Innovation and serendipity, they're both extremely social – so much is bound up with how people rub along together. This book places human beings, with all their weird foibles, at the centre of the science of serendipity. The 'science' goes like this: get hold of the right type of person and give them a brief that is both constraining yet has plenty of room for exploration. Then unleash them on a quest for provocative insight and ensure they do experimental stuff rather than talk about clever stuff. Above all they need good humour to pick themselves up, dust themselves down and try again. With this in mind, this is how the book flows:

- In Chapter 1, *The Protagonist*, we explore the qualities of a successful innovator within a corporate environment. I've called this person a 'Captain One Minute, Pirate the Next'. They are both a visionary and a maverick. We'll unpick their psychological make-up and understand why they are so good at exploiting serendipity.

- In Chapter 2, *The Quest for Provocation*, we look at how busy executives get out of the office and into the habit of making fresh connections. This is a process that can be deliberately managed and is the raw material for serendipity. Think of it as a practical exploration of how to 'prepare the mind' so that chance will favour it.

- In Chapter 3, *Making Ideas Real*, we take a detailed look at the innovator's weapon of choice. The ability to make a series of mini experiments that build out and prove an idea is essential to exploiting serendipity. We look at the philosophy and practice of how to make ideas real from their initial formation all the way through to a prototype, pilot, launch and even beyond.

- In Chapter 4, *Collision Course*, we take a look at something that's often underrated but is in fact a prime mover of serendipity. We explore how the physical space around us drives us to connect ideas and gives us the confidence to develop them all the way to launch.

- In Chapter 5, *Battling the Corporate Machine*, we look at the real-politik of innovation; what kind of combat awaits the innovator as they battle the corporate machine? This chapter, full of battlefield stories, is a survivor's guide to making the most of serendipity.

The message of the book is that you can make your own luck if you're prepared to work hard and be bold.

Of course, there is a British bias to the book – I live in London, write in British English and like warm beer – but I do believe that innovation affects us all. It's a global phenomenon. I've lived in Asia and the Middle East and worked pretty much everywhere. There are some clear cultural differences in the way we do business that most of us are familiar with, but innovation is a basic instinct and like arguing, laughing or canoodling; we all do it much the same way wherever we are.

In this book I use the word 'company' and 'organisation' pretty much interchangeably. The terms 'customer' and 'consumer' do mean different things (buyer and user) and I've tried to use them accurately.

Finally, innovation is allergic to overthinking. Often the concept that has been worked and reworked, debated and re-debated, researched and re-researched, morphs into something utterly mediocre. Along the way the spark of an idea got throttled. Innovation is a 'doing' sport where diving in and trying things out is better than thinking or talking for too long, so I have deliberately biased the content towards action rather than analysis. Where I can, I tease out the stresses and strains executives have felt when trying to do things differently – I hope this gives you comfort that you're not alone.

It takes 2 hours and 15 minutes to read this book – that includes a break for a cup of tea. Or you can finish it in a fortnight by reading for 10 minutes a day. After you've put it down for the last time, I hope you're going to grab the phone, call your colleagues and get stuck into some of the exercises and activities I'm going to share with you. Above all, you must not be afraid to try; accept that you won't get everything right and that failure will shape a greater victory very soon.

To find out more go to www.whatifinnovation.com

66

'Serendipity is looking for a needle in a haystack and finding the farmer's daughter.'

Julius H. Comroe

1

The Protagonist

'Captain One Minute, Pirate the Next'

In 30 seconds

If you only had 30 seconds I'd tell you:

All innovation is powered by human emotion: anger, paranoia or ambition.

◆

A great innovation process will never compensate for poor innovation people.

◆

The profile of an ideal innovator is a 'Captain One Minute, Pirate the Next' – someone who respects their organisation but doesn't revere it.

◆

They are unreasonably ambitious, relentlessly pushing the boundaries in a way that doesn't always make sense.

◆

But they're not egomaniacs; they know when to shut up and listen.

◆

They research as little as possible, and are confident enough in their own judgement to back themselves.

◆

They are team workers, but more than that, they are collaborators.

◆

They're socially skilled and able to guide others between an expansive world of ideas and a reductive world of decisions.

◆

They're not necessarily creative, but they are good finishers.

A rt has been the Chief Innovation Officer of a global bank for the past year. He oversees a pipeline of about 20 innovation initiatives around the world, each one managed by a team working within its own P&L. Increasingly, Art's efforts to navigate the company's internal processes and nudge these initiatives to launch are met with indifference and, in some cases, hostility. 'It's like I'm putting a baby in the boxing ring', Art says of the ideas it's his job to champion. 'These projects need more investment and protection.' Art has started to wonder how much his bank really wants to innovate and – in his darker moments – why he took the job in the first place.

Lillian is the Head of Marketing for one of a global pharmaceutical company's blockbuster brands. With only 8 years of patent-protected revenue under its belt, Lillian knows her focus should be on innovating new ways to extend the drug's reach. But she just can't seem to carve out the time. 'I feel crushed by the constant need to cover off the senior management', she says. 'Every day some junior staffer is asking me to prepare a one-page summary for someone important somewhere. What I need to be doing is getting out of this office and into the marketplace, where I can make a real difference.' Instead, she and her colleagues spend most of their time trapped in meetings or creating spreadsheets to justify the company's innovation investments.

John runs the Innovation Centre for a large multinational packaged goods company. He drives development across all regions of a group of brands, and oversees a large team of research scientists, packaging developers and marketers. Recently, following a particularly rocky product launch, his company mandated an 'innovation protocol'. Now each project must pass through a series of gates, with each gate culminating in an all-day review meeting – an event that demands weeks of paperwork and preparation. The top brass fly in for these meetings, which are scheduled up to a year in advance. John doesn't mind thinking things through, but in his gut he knows innovation doesn't work like this. 'It's as if the organisation has these great grinding wheels of decision-making that slowly turn', he says. 'I'm just a little wheel called innovation and I can't seem to find a way to synchronise with the big wheel.' To make matters worse, John's people are starting to jump ship for smaller, less process-driven competitors.

Stories like these are not uncommon. Dig behind innovation and you'll find people who are frustrated, restless and ambitious. It's this human energy that drives innovation; people sparking off people. Rarely, if ever, does anyone claim that it was the process or the organisational structure that 'won it'. The protagonists who pull and push new things through a big company need to have some special qualities to survive the kind of combat they're about to face. They need an unreasonable dose of ambition. They need to be humble enough to know they don't have all the answers and yet confident enough to back themselves. They need to be not just great team-workers but also collaborators – and they need to be able to make things happen.

So who is crazy enough to want this job?

'Captain One Minute, Pirate the Next'

Most successful big-company innovators I meet, whether Chief Innovation Officers, innovation team members or people without an innovation job title but who are tackling a big change project for the first time, have something in common: they respect the organisation they work for, but they don't revere it. As innovators, they want their businesses to do better, but at the same time they are dissatisfied with the status quo. There's a kind of 'love–hate' thing going on. But too much love and an innovator becomes an ineffective 'yes-man'. Too much hate and he or she ends up an ineffective loner.

It's a delicate balancing act. I describe someone who effectively manages it as a 'Captain One Minute, Pirate the Next'. One minute the innovation leader is the Captain, the passionate man-with-the-plan, standing tall on the bridge of the ship and inspiring us all to go 'this way'. But the next time you meet, the Captain has morphed into a Pirate. This time he or she is down in the boiler room, sleeves rolled up, shipmates gathered around, using all of his or her cunning to shortcut a process, to subvert the system. Now our protagonist is asking really challenging questions: 'What if we did it differently? What if we ripped up the way things are done around here? What if?'

So one minute an innovation leader is stubbornly sticking to the big picture; the next he or she is telling you not to sweat the small stuff. I think this intriguing mix of vision and cunning comes from the fact that successful innovators are fixated by outcomes. They are highly motivated to make change happen – so much so that they're often less bothered about how they get there.

These are the qualities of a 'Captain One Minute, Pirate the Next':

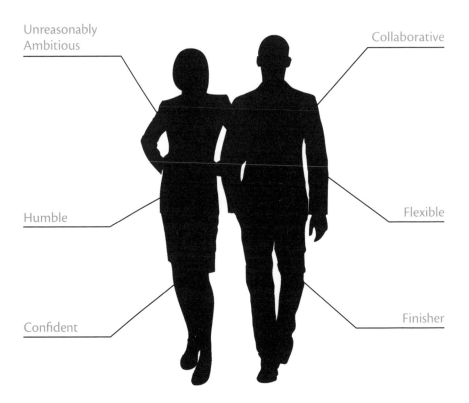

Unreasonably Ambitious

Collaborative

Humble

Flexible

Confident

Finisher

To be clear, I've never met anyone who scored high on all the traits of a 'Captain One Minute, Pirate the Next'. The key is to recognise where you or your team are weak and either work at developing new skills or find people to compensate.

Unreasonably Ambitious: **Always Pushing the Boundaries**

Innovation starts with someone throwing a stone a long way. Innovators are good at this. They know that stretch goals – aiming beyond your own limits – create better performance. They know that their team, brand or organisation needs to work towards a picture of something that's truly exciting. If this picture doesn't exist then it's very hard to do anything other than incremental improvements – small twists and tweaks.

Innovation is literally thrilling. The ambition of an innovation leader and his or her team needs a degree of unreasonableness to it, a feeling of 'Wow, you've got to be kidding – how the hell are we going to do that?' Successful innovators in large companies aren't afraid to scare people shitless. When they find themselves surrounded by doubters, they develop a big fat grin – they know they're on the right track.

Axe, or Lynx depending on where in the world you live, is one of Unilever's leading brands and a good example of this approach. The Axe line-up of grooming products includes body sprays, deodorants, antiperspirants, shower gels, shampoos and styling products and claims to 'give guys confidence when it comes to getting the girl'.

In 2002, inspired by a scene from *The Matrix* in which the protagonist is offered the choice of a life-changing pill, newly appointed brand director at Unilever, Neil Munn, created the 'Republic of Axe'. This was a bold new brand culture within Unilever that had its own laddish identity. 'We needed walls', said Munn. 'Inside was our vibe, our beat.' Fuelled with the excitement of being a renegade team, bent on helping young men get ahead in the mating game, Axe has enjoyed strong growth each year with wave after wave of award-winning advertising driving successful new products (such as Anti-Hangover shower gel that 'gets the night out of your system').

This innovation journey, of course, hasn't been all plain sailing. In its wake are discarded and banned TV commercials. More than once Unilever has apologised online for going 'too far' with Axe, thus guaranteeing cult status amongst young men the world over. How did Unilever, a megasized company famous for sensible household brands such as Surf, Persil and Knorr, manage to spawn such a maverick tribe?

> **"**
>
> *To be entrepreneurial in a large company you can't be afraid to leave*

Munn, who left the brand in 2006, says 'I had to defend the brand, and my boss (the President of Unilever Deodorants category) had to give me air cover. Without this we wouldn't have had the space and the confidence to flex our muscles and experiment – the brand is all about pushing it.' Munn also created an ambitious and powerful allegorical device that became iconic throughout the business: instead of just 'joining the team', new members had to agree to 'take the red pill'. This is a commitment to rapid and audacious decision-making that is played out daily in the Axe Republic (i.e. brand offices throughout the world) where decisions aren't supposed to be safe. In a characteristic move, Munn once presented his annual plan on video while having a massage; an unusual move, but entirely appropriate to the brand.

Finally, Munn admits to several moments where he thought he'd pushed the mothership too far but 'to be entrepreneurial in a large company you can't be afraid to leave', says Munn, 'the dynamic in megacorps isn't about fast decision-making, so our view was that we were going to just get on with things unless we were told to stop, which we never were'.

Large companies are like supertankers; they have a need to be predictable because their owners don't like surprises. They are very good at moving in one direction at a steady pace but often poor at turning quickly and exploring uncharted seas. The story of Axe is highly instructive. It tells us that innovation needs a rebellious band bent on doing things differently; think of it as an anticulture. As these rebel teams push hard and fast, whatever they propose will sound unreasonably ambitious.

The story of Axe/Lynx is also a reminder that it can be more powerful to express innovation goals in human terms rather than complex business terminology. Think of Steve Jobs telling his team they were going to 'put a dent in the universe'. Or one of my favourite examples, Victoria Beckham. When starting her career with the Spice Girls (as Posh Spice), she promised the world she was going to be 'as famous as Persil Automatic'. Persil, a global detergent megabrand, was a great benchmark. If she had chosen to be as famous as a well-known movie star her goal would have sounded arrogant. The choice of Persil Automatic is easy to understand, has a charm to it, is memorable and sounds authentic. Business leaders take note – lessons come from the most unlikely places.

The overall challenge is for an innovation leader to articulate his or her goals in a way that:

- Is expressed in everyday, blunt language

- Is measurable or 'benchmark-able'

- Appeals to basic human instincts: to win, to pulverise the enemy, to make the world a better place, to get outrageously rich.

So to lead innovation successfully, does the protagonist need to be a charismatic, larger-than-life character? My answer, of course, is *'No'*. Many who have successfully innovated in large companies work hard to manage their network and allow others to take the plaudits. Innovation leaders can be behind-the-scenes people who think deeply about the next move.

Humble: Knowing When to Shut Up and Listen

Innovators need a healthy balance of confidence and self-doubt. They need big ambition but a small ego. There is nothing more dangerous than the know-it-all; the guy or girl who has all the answers.

So, innovators need to know when to shut up and start listening. They need to be opinionated enough to form a hypothesis but humble enough to know that their idea might not be the best, or that someone else will probably be able to make it better. Innovators are good at alternatives – they get used to putting aside the front-runner of an idea to search for another, and then another. This means they can't get too attached to ideas. They need to be constantly challenging themselves: *'What if there's a better way, let's keep going, just one more idea ...'*

We need good listeners who will consider alternative opinions. But we don't want 'flip-floppers' – people who just jump from the last opinion they heard to the next. This is a genuinely stressful issue for innovators; *'How long do I keep listening? When do I say "stop – that's enough opinion, I've made my mind up and we're going this way"?'* In my experience, people at work appreciate listening and action in equal measure. So don't be afraid to stop listening and start doing.

And it's not enough just to be a good listener; you need a reputation for it too. This is because innovators need to attract ideas from all over their organisation. The experience of kicking an idea around with the innovation team has to be positive. If the team has a poor reputation for listening, it will get little engagement or traction. So we need to apply the same sort of standards to the 'experience' of innovation dialogue as we do, say, to the customer experience of the products we sell. Just as a waiter in a restaurant 'gives good service', innovators have to 'give good listening'.

Much of our work at ?What If! involves working with clients who are fundamentally different to their consumers. Typical dynamics are middle-aged men innovating for younger female consumers, digitally savvy executives innovating for the technologically illiterate, or clever graduates innovating for hardworking retirees. In these cases it's critical to just shut up, look, listen and learn from your customers.

This is easier said than done. Accompanying a young single mum on a shopping expedition, one of our gallant 'gentleman' clients inadvertently revealed he'd held the woman's shopping bags on the bus ride home and discussed his recent skiing holiday. It seemed to us that he was nervous meeting this customer and compensated by talking too much. As a result he wasted his time. The temptation to be nice often overwhelms the need to shut up and just melt into the background.

Confident: **Believing Enough to Back Yourself**

Innovation is a combat sport. You need the hide of a rhinoceros to take the kind of battering you will surely face to get ideas across the line in most companies. This isn't a job for people easily crushed by the opinions of others.

Much of the innovation leader's job is to engage people at the top with ideas that don't yet have a robust financial story, or to engage with people who are cynical even about the need for innovation. Innovation can be as unnerving as it is exciting. This environment rules out rookies and favours those with battle-scars, who have confidence in their own judgement and who are not afraid to back themselves.

Confidence isn't the same as having a giant ego. Most giant egos meet a giant career crash at some stage. Confidence is a quiet thing born out of a belief that what you're doing is 'right'. What powers innovators is a belief that the world could be a better place, even in a small way, and that they have the means to make this happen.

Let's take a peek behind the scenes of a company that eschews conventional research and works hard to develop 'belief' in what they are doing.

ASOS is a £480m fast-growing online fashion retailer. If you don't know ASOS already, then go online now and check them out. Use your laptop but try shopping ASOS on your smartphone as so many customers do. Explore Marketplace, where independent boutiques can sell their latest lines; and Fashion Finder, where ASOS directs you to brands and products they don't sell but they think you'll like. So here's the hottest fashion business

– the second most visited fashion retail site globally – and they're routing you elsewhere?

ASOS uploads about 1500 new items per week onto its site. Suppliers fight to get listed and the turnaround time to prepare, shoot and upload each item is a dizzying 8 minutes. The range is vast; the corridors at ASOS London HQ are swarming with the latest hot new items and models queuing in Make Up. ASOS reaches fashion conscious teens in 100+ countries – in 2011 ASOS became the biggest fashion site in Australia and New Zealand with no shops, no advertising and not even any people.

ASOS finds itself at the confluence of two megatrends: the rapid growth of teenage buying power in developing countries and the unstoppable march of the smartphone. The minute teenagers have to queue, get bored, can't sleep, wait for a bus or even sit on the loo, then out comes the smartphone. And now there's a shop in the palm of their hand with new lines everyday, and guess what, ASOS deliver for free anywhere in the world and if things don't fit you can return them to ASOS at no charge.

Nick Robertson is the CEO at ASOS and it's his creation. He doesn't need external research to tell him what people want. He's lucky to have most of his employees as typical customers and they're free to tweet about the company. As Nick says 'I read blogs, staff tweets, other tweets – all the insight is there, all the strategy we need.'

This confidence in getting it right for the customer is all pervasive: 'We don't have strategy here', Robertson says. 'We have a loose idea, it's not set in stone. If you start with the customer and what they want then you can build the financials around that.'

Robertson adds that 'It's ironic; at ASOS the more we give (for free) the more we get back. Fashion Finder and Marketplace – easy decisions if you build from the heart. Other companies would have found this very hard, called it disruptive.' Sincere belief in doing what's right for the customer has enabled ASOS to innovate and turn retail conventions upside down. Robertson clearly sees ASOS more as a movement than a 'retailer': 'ASOS is as much a retailer as it is a publisher as it is an enabler of fashion'.

Much of Robertson's confidence comes from the fact that he trusts his gut. He's had to make a lot of decisions without relying on market research. He's fortunate in having so many customers as staff and that his business model enables him to remove slow moving lines more or less immediately. But the principle is universal: the more an innovator is able to make decisions based on his or her own judgement, the more instinctive he or she becomes. Some organisations just have too much money. They default to researching things that don't need to be researched; instead they need someone to make a decision.

'Believe in yourself. You spend your life talking to people and everyone has a different opinion. It's quite easy to get distracted by that. You have to know where you are going. Look into the horizon and that is the destination. All the time you are going to have people telling you it's wrong but sometimes trust yourself.'

Nick Robertson, from Jaffer and Bordell (2011)

Collaborative: **Embracing Diverse and External Factors**

There is a critical distinction to be made between teamwork and collaboration, but these words are often used interchangeably. Sure, innovation needs people to pull together as a team, but what it really needs is for people to be able to collaborate, often with contacts and organisations outside the company – maybe competitors, suppliers, maybe even people the company has never considered talking to.

Consider any team sport – winning is often down to teamwork. But to say that players 'collaborate' to win sounds odd. That's because teamwork has boundaries (the duration of the game is fixed, the size of the pitch is fixed …), it has rules, players have positions and what constitutes victory is normally pretty clear. But collaboration operates in a different environment where the boundaries and rules aren't clear. In fact the rules unfold as the project progresses and collaborating parties don't have a clear idea of what victory looks like – it's something they feel their way towards.

> *Too often teamwork looks like polite people making minimal progress, whereas collaboration is an altogether more robust concept*

Too often teamwork looks like polite people making minimal progress, whereas collaboration is an altogether more robust concept that doesn't tolerate mediocrity and drives step change.

Collaboration is an admission that you and your team haven't got all the answers. True collaboration means that all parties open up a bit. There's a tacit implication in attempting to collaborate; you're saying 'I can't do this alone. I don't have all the answers. Can we mix our thinking up and see what happens?' So allowing oneself to feel vulnerable is part and parcel of the collaborator's way.

So what does collaboration look like in practice? Firstly, collaborators really value diversity. They surround themselves with the kind of 'difference' that will enable serendipitous encounters. Innovators have a high tolerance for people from different cultures and skill sets. They generally have a wide circle of friends, acquaintances and interests. They're curious, occasionally eccentric people. Secondly, collaboration in practice has no boundaries. Innovators often face outwards, more so than anyone else in the organisation. They work hard to foster links outside their business and should be encouraged to do so. If they are in the office too much, they're not doing their job.

A good buddy of mine helped save a life recently, and if all goes well he'll save many more. Dave Green is President of Boston-based Harvard Bioscience. They're the guys who developed and manufactured the kit that helped create the world's first regenerated trachea implant in a 36 year old man suffering from 'inoperable' and terminal tracheal cancer (he'd been given two weeks to live). The surgery took place in June 2011 in Sweden. As we go to print, the patient is approaching his one year anniversary of the surgery.

The science in a nutshell is this: harvest stem cells from hip; create spongy plastic replica trachea; baste with cells for 2 days while they seed; grow and merge; remove cancerous trachea and replace with new. A few weeks later patient leaves hospital. A death sentence reversed. How mighty is the promise of innovation!

Dave tells his innovation story like this:

'Back in 2004 I began to get interested in the power of stem cells. I read up about them and got myself rigged up to just about every scientific journal, conference and mailing list imaginable. I started chairing the Harvard Business School Healthcare Alumni Annual Conference, something that enabled me to talk about my interest, meet many experts in the field and learn about the business of medicine like FDA approvals and government reimbursement. I have no background in medicine, but eventually I figured our company could create the machinery to build highly fibrous body parts like a trachea. I reached out to Professor Paolo Macchiarini, the surgeon pioneering in this field and suggested we could help. Shortly after his warm email reply I was on a plane to Italy. The next year is a blur of pulling together specialists from all over the world – the team literally included people from Italy, Spain, UK, Iran, Germany, Sweden, Iceland and the US. When we eventually did the first regenerated trachea transplant there were over 20 people in the operating theatre and many more outside. Each of them have played a critical role in the innovation, none of us could have done it alone'.

Note how many external points of reference Green refers to in his story: literature, the internet, a conference, the world-renowned surgeon and ultimately a small army of technicians during the operation itself. All the protagonists to the story were figuring out their role as they went along, none was sure of what they would get out of it or where the story would end up. Green got himself out of the office, camped out on the right person's doorstep, jumped on a plane and did whatever it took to collaborate.

Flexible: Navigate Between Expansive and Reductive Thinking

There are two worlds an innovator needs to switch between. Let's call one Planet Expand and the other Planet Reduce. During the innovation process we are orbiting one planet and then another. While we're orbiting Planet Expand we're seeking out stimulus, we're looking for alternatives and we're having ideas. We've deliberately dropped all constraints and are tossing ideas around. This can be a lot of fun but too long orbiting Planet Expand drives most people nuts.

At some stage we have to put the boosters on and escape the gravitational pull of Planet Expand and head off towards Planet Reduce, sometimes known as the 'Real World'. This is a different place altogether. Now we're using our experience to reduce the amount of choice we have generated.

Switching between these planets might happen several times during the course of a 5-minute conversation and potentially hundreds of times over the life of an innovation project. Below is a typical innovation project process:

Agree business growth goals

▼

Develop innovation mandate

▼

Team selection and development of
accountability process

▼

Opportunity assessment

▼

Data search and insight gather

▼

Idea generation and selection

▼

Proposition development, prototypes and pilots

▼

Build the investment case, secure supply, technology
and distribution

▼

Stakeholder management and launch agreement

This process looks pretty logical. But don't kid yourself. Innovation isn't a neat and tidy linear journey as diagrams like these can have you believe. You might find yourself joining halfway through the journey, your money runs out at unexpected junctures, the brief changes and the process is redrawn. These are the realities of an innovation process. And while this is going on you're constantly switching between Planet Expand and Planet Reduce. Managing the discipline of innovation process against this potentially chaotic backdrop needs people with highly developed interpersonal skills who can guide the conversations between these expansive and reductive states.

Signalling is a term we coined at ?What If! and it is a simple linguistic technique used to navigate the switch between these two worlds of innovation.

Once you are aware of the need to signal, it's easy to do and can have a dramatic effect on the outcome of an intimate conversation or group dialogue. Let's eavesdrop on an imaginary conversation between a store manager and his staff:

Signal (Manager):	*'Let's forget all about how we work for a minute, what could we do to increase staff engagement?'*
Response (Staff):	*'We could swap jobs within the store once a year, just for a day'*
Signal:	*'That's interesting, what else could we do?'*
Response:	*'We could swap jobs with the top brass!'*
Signal:	*'OK, lets push that idea'*
Response:	*'The top brass could do our jobs and we could mark them and give them feedback at the end of the day!'*

Signal: *'We need to close this down now, who has got a proposal about how we could test the idea fast?*

Response: *'I think we can have one department do a job swap, if that works we'll do it across the store, then if that works we'll invite the top brass to join in.'*

Signalling alerts others as to how you want them to react. Notice how the signals in the dialogue above expanded, then contracted the conversation?

There is a critical moment in every creative conversation and it goes like this:

> *'I've got this thought, it's not formed, frankly it might sound a little weird but can you help me build it?'*

This is a huge signal. It is saying PLEASE DON'T PISS ON THIS IDEA. Ignore this at your peril.

The other signal that really helps is to reassure that the expansion phase won't go on forever:

> *'Guys, let's kick this around together, I want us to get 20 different and radical ideas on the table, when we've done that we'll have a break and then come back and figure out the one or two we want to take forward.'*

Think of signalling as the indicator lights on your car. They tell other cars of your intentions. Without them things can get messy. We've all experienced trying to 'close down' a debate while the lone genius drones on with their stream of creativity – very frustrating. Equally annoying is Mr Worry who keeps asking for proof when the rest of the room is exploring a world of possibilities. Once you've been driving for a while, then signalling is automatic. It's the same in the creative process – soon you won't even realise you're doing it.

Finisher: A Relentless Drive to 'Get It Over the Line'

Any battle-hardened innovation veteran will tell you that 'having the idea was the easy bit, getting it to market nearly killed me'. Innovators need to be good finishers. They need to mentally lock on the endgame, get their heads down and charge.

The most frequent question I get asked about people in innovation roles in large companies is whether they need to be creative people. Creativity does have an important role to play in innovation. Making the connections that no one has seen lies at the heart of serendipity. But while creative people throw up a lot of options, they don't always close them down. A large organisation has a limited capacity to deal with options; too many initiatives and everything grinds to a halt.

So the answer is 'No', creativity isn't a prerequisite of an innovator as long as they realise the extent of their limitations. Someone who can get things done and can call on creative people to add flair – that's the ideal combination. The alternative, a creative starter who surrounds themselves with good finishers might work in a start-up organisation but becomes very frustrating in a large organisation as initiatives pile up.

Part of being a good finisher is being a good 'unblocker'. Innovators are the master plumbers of the business world. They understand the political realities of their organisation and they know who they need in their pocket to make things move smoothly through the system. The best innovators I have worked with lament the amount of process they have to deal with. They are frustrated with the avalanche of 'internal stuff' that occupies much of their day. But they have developed coping mechanisms; they're good at keeping everyone focused on the human side of innovation – the customer. A good innovator keeps us focused on what we're trying to achieve. As a result, roadblocks disappear.

> **"**
>
> *Someone who can get things done and can call on creative people to add flair – that's the ideal combination*

The spectre of a stalled innovation process is depressingly common. Everyone in every business has at some point hit their head against the wall, whilst offering a silent prayer that the floor would open up and take them away to a more tranquil environment. This sense of frustration that things don't move fast enough is disabling but it's also inevitable, like acne is to a teenager. The only way to cope is to take a deep breath, get over it and make an 'unblocking plan'.

Sometimes we need a dramatic intervention to unblock the pipes. A client of ours, a large hospital, had got stuck whilst designing a new system for incoming patients. Some were walking wounded but most were returning for regular treatment. The hospital reception area was a mess, it was noisy and disorganised – a terrible first experience for any patient.

We'd been trying to crack the problem for months, but there were many stakeholders with conflicting views. The junior doctors wanted the consulting rooms to be used on a first come, first use basis. The senior doctors wanted their own consulting rooms regardless of whether they were working or not. The receptionists wanted to recruit more help getting samples to the pathology lab on the sixth floor (the internal post took 24 hours) but the management wanted to reduce headcount.

We had reached an impasse but fortunately the hospital had a clever 'Master Plumber' on the team. The next meeting, which I think we'd all been dreading, turned out to be a great success. Our Master Plumber opened the meeting by introducing us to three patients. They stood in front of us and calmly told their story about just how bad the hospital experience had been, how it had affected their health and how their families had been affected as well.

This was a moving experience, and it was clear that cracking the problem was a lot more important than squabbling amongst ourselves. Soon a new mood of cooperation took hold. Within weeks we had hired a runner to speed the pathology reports, we started training receptionists as phlebotomists (so they could take blood when nursing staff were overloaded) and, whereas previously the senior doctors demanded their own consulting rooms, they now agreed to a flexible, shared arrangement.

Innovation is a very practical subject. There are flashes of creativity but mainly there are long dark nights hammering out just how something is going to work. This demands an endurance and an alignment around a single goal. A good finisher is good at spotting who they need onside and figuring ways to unblock the system. They're realists – rather than get bent out of shape over the inertia of the 'system', they get their heads down and charge. They're relentless in their pursuit of getting innovation 'over the line'.

"

'Concerning all acts of initiative (and creation), there is one elementary truth the ignorance of which kills countless ideas and splendid plans: that the moment one definitely commits oneself, then providence moves too.'

W. H. Murray. *The Scottish Himalayan Expedition* (1951)

Let's Get Practical

So how much of a 'Captain One Minute, Pirate the Next' are you? Don't even try to answer this question alone – get some help from people who know you well and aren't afraid to tell you the truth. Below are several questions that are prompts for discussion. But don't beat yourself up if the scores are low on some questions – few individuals have all these qualities.

* How have you articulated the ambition for your business (or team, division, department ...)? Be honest – does your heart beat faster when you explain the things in the world you're going to put right? Are your hands itching to leave their pockets and punch the air? Many people give up too easily when answering this question: 'How can my business possibly be exciting?' You need to answer this question. Without a sense of audacity and passion innovation will never take off.

* Do you 'give good listening'? Innovation needs people with humility and empathy. This comes from and is evidenced by your ability to listen. You may never have surveyed your colleagues on your reputation for this – many executives haven't, but understanding your credibility as a 'listener' is critical.

* Do you 'go with your gut' or keep asking for more research before making a decision? To what extent do you 'back yourself'?

* Are you more external or internal facing? Maybe think back to your last innovation project or engagement – how many people outside of your organisation did you seek inspiration from and collaborate with?

* Can you navigate between an expansive and reductive process? Do you know when to switch from creative to analytic mode, or vice versa?

* Finally, are you realistic about your ability to finish things off?

Note the question isn't about your ability to finish things but your awareness of your ability. If you're a poor finisher don't lose heart – surround yourself with people who are good at it.

2

The Quest for Provocation

The Deliberate Management of Inspiration

In **30** seconds

If you only had 30 seconds I'd tell you:

Innovation is fuelled by new insight – a deep
understanding of why people do what they do.

◆

A good insight is like a well-fertilised garden – it can't
help but generate green shoot ideas.

◆

Insight is created by the serendipitous collision of
provocative observations.

◆

In most large organisations it's all too easy to get stuck
in a rut with little opportunity to get provoked.

◆

There are tried and tested 'lenses of provocation'. Work
through these and you can unearth a multitude of
stimulating new observations.

◆

The quest for provocation is always uncomfortable; take
courage, get out of the office and go to the margins of
your market.

◆

You can't set out on this quest for provocation without
preparation. It's true, chance really does favour the
'prepared mind'.

There I was, crammed into a hotel room with the senior operations management team of a giant global insurance company. These were the guys who looked after how information flowed around the company, how call centres were managed and how technology supported various insurance products. We called room service. Not because we were hungry, but because this hotel was famous for its room service. There were over 40 separate service standards dictating how to deliver a burger and fries to a room.

This kind of highly regulated system normally produces 'cookie cutter' service – employees learn the drill but seem incapable of going off script when an unusual request or situation presents itself. We were there to learn how this hotel could deal with the weirdest requests. So there we were, ordering burgers with every imaginable topping, cancelling orders and generally making a pain in the arse of ourselves and all the time the waiter was smiling, taking it in his stride.

So somehow, the hotel had cracked a way to have service standards and allow the waiters to use their intelligence to overrule the system when required. It was a trait this insurance company desperately wanted their people to have. The insurance call centre staff were frequently criticised for 'acting like robots'; they were inflexible and lacked empathy with customers.

The next morning we met in a very different environment; a café in a run-down housing estate. We paired off and spent the day with its low or no income residents. These were the kind of people the insurance company's research programme dismissed as 'off-strategy'. We went inside their homes, met their friends and observed how they spent their money. We learnt that they lent and borrowed among themselves, using new-at-the-time services like Wonga and PayPal. If there was a disaster, it got sorted out within the family, not through an insurance company. Banks and insurers simply weren't on their radar.

Later in the day we all gathered in a small terraced house to share our observations. The homeowner asked the executives to take their shoes off when they entered. We spent the session squeezed into a small room discussing our findings in stockinged feet. I think the 'shoes off' thing made a big difference. In some way it was a great leveller and big signal that we were a long way from the office.

In our quest to provoke these executives, we also introduced them to a convicted insurance fraudster, people who didn't 'believe' in insurance on religious and ethical grounds, and even employees of their own company who had been buying competitors' insurance products.

The rich mix of provocative insight gleaned from the exercises above was unlike anything the insurance company had done before. For years they had commissioned the same type of research amongst the same type of customers, even using the same researchers. But the experience of the excellent room service, the disenfranchised homeowners, the fraudster and the insurance non-believer had shaken free a stream of insights and ideas. Eventually the Operations Team developed new ideas that affected many parts of the organisation; who they hired, how complaints were dealt with, a new 'common sense' basic training scheme and much more.

The serendipity formula at its most basic level is 'garbage in = garbage out'. In other words, if you fill your head with the same old things, then the same old things will come out. Provocation is the deliberate quest to have your view of the world challenged. It's the search for a new stimulus that tells us why our assumptions about the world might be wrong. A rich mix of provocation is the raw material for serendipity and a springboard for innovation. The quest for provocation takes us out of the office to experience all the things our customers experience. It takes us to meet people who have an extreme relationship with our products and to experience others who've cracked similar problems but in other markets.

The quest for provocation is by definition uncomfortable. It takes real balls to design a journey with the purpose of challenging the status quo. We need to feel both inspired and a little threatened as a result. Provocation also has a competitive edge. Do you know whether your competitors are working from the same data that you are? Or are they looking in different, more stimulating places and making more connections? Provocation – and the clues, connections, and insights it generates – is fundamental to innovation and competition.

66

'Creativity is just connecting things. When you ask creative people how they did something, they feel a little guilty because they didn't really do it, they just saw something. It seemed obvious to them after a while ... they were able to connect experiences they've had and synthesize new things.'

Steve Jobs in a *Wired* interview with Wolf (1996)

Stuck in a Rut

It's a fact of life. The same route to work, the same coffee from the corner shop, the same faces, the same issues at work – we can't help but get good at repeating today what worked yesterday. Once we've invested heavily in the past, our neuronal pathways get burnt into motorways set into deep ravines, with ever-fewer exits.

At a collective level, whole organisations can lose their peripheral vision and get stuck in a rut. History is littered with stories of clever people engaging in groupthink with disastrous results. In 2012 the Kodak Eastman Company filed for Chapter 11 bankruptcy protection, its digital camera business having finally given up in the face of left-field entrants like Apple's iPhone. Contrary to popular belief, Kodak hadn't been blind to innovation. It had a surprising string of firsts: the first digital camera, the first Wi-Fi camera and the first touchscreen camera. Its profits and market share were high, even after digital cameras took off. But even though its executives could hear the train coming, they didn't move fast enough, they didn't move off the crossing – and when they did, it was too late. An anonymous Kodak executive recently said that 'The difference between [Kodak's] traditional business and digital was so great. The tempo is different. The kinds of skills you need are different. [The management] would tell you that they wanted change, but they didn't want to force pain on the organisation.'

In the same way, Encyclopaedia Britannica failed to capitalise on the digital revolution. First sold in 1768 in Scotland and then from 1901 headquartered in the US, sales of the 32-volume tome had dwindled from a peak of 120,000 in 1990 to only 4000 just ten years later. Sales of the printed set ceased in 2012.

Like Kodak, it wasn't that Encyclopaedia Britannica was blind to the digital revolution. They launched EBlast, a curated web directory of sites when no one knew what a web directory was. They experimented with linking their content to current news stories on the net; just click from the news article through to Encyclopaedia Britannica for more content, was the idea.

The problem was that Encyclopaedia Britannica was in a rut. They had such an authoritative editorial board, such august contributors (Nobel prize winners amongst others) and so much history in diligently collecting and editing the facts that they couldn't see that it was 'access' and not the quality of the content providers that had become the main thing.

Encyclopaedia Britannica was always an aspirational purchase, mainly by working class parents who wanted a better life for their kids – opportunities they never had. They switched to buying PCs (about the same price as the 32 volume set) that came with free Encarta encyclopaedia software. Still Encyclopaedia Britannica clung to the notion that content was king even though many of the weighty books were never taken off the shelves. Today Wikipedia has the power of vast numbers of editors and the ability to immediately update. Clearly these are huge benefits compared to rarely edited paper books. But it wasn't technology that killed Encyclopaedia Britannica, it was their failure to recognise that the voice of a thousand 'Joe Publics' is as important as a single Nobel laureate.

All the answers were outside Kodak and Encyclopaedia Britannica's office door, but understandably the fear of cannibalisation of their sunken capital limited their ability to think and act flexibly.

They are not alone. Tesco is a £72bn global retailer with 6234 stores in 14 countries. Fuelled by years of spectacular results they opened Fresh & Easy supermarkets in Nevada, California and Arizona in 2007 and 2008. Tesco researched the market diligently with over 60 families who opened up their homes and shopping habits to its Brit executives for two weeks. But initial sales results were disappointing; somehow the store layout and the product mix wasn't working.

Looking back, Tim Mason (Chief Executive Officer and President of Fresh & Easy since 2006) candidly admits in an interview with William Kay (2009) that the mistake was to not look in customers' garages. If they had done so they would have found chest freezers stocked with bulk-bought produce purchased on special offer. 'There's less loyalty in the American market', said Mason. 'A Brit has to hear it a few times before you accept that people make up their mind where to go each week when they check out the special offers round the kitchen table'.

So even the most sophisticated operator can get stuck in a rut. To get properly provoked we need to be creative and audacious in our approach, but we also need to plan it carefully. None of us have infinite time or money to blow on getting endless provocative stimuli.

So where shall the quest take us first?

The Answer: **Under Your Nose?**

Sometimes all the provocation you need is so close you can't see it. Sometimes your own customers or colleagues can tell you your innovation strategy – in minutes – so ask them first. You might just save yourself a lot of time and money.

> In the late 1990s easyJet, now Europe's leading no-frills airline, had a problem with punctuality. This was a very big issue at the time, as the reputational damage could have impacted an

upcoming stock market float. But all the information easyJet needed was under its nose.

Working with the easyJet team, we assembled all the people who contributed to servicing an airplane at the gate. There were a surprisingly large number of people in the room representing a wide variety of expertise, nationalities, unions and employers. Clearly this was their first opportunity to build better ideas together. We asked the people in the room what was slowing things down and what they would do if 'they were in charge'. They told us that they often waited for the pilot to finish communicating with the control tower before they could radio up to the cockpit and ask about catering and fuel requirements. They also told us about how precisely you needed to park the unloading, fuelling and catering vehicles around the airplane. People, of course, tend to enjoy listing the problems 'other people' have caused.

After a very short time we had a massive amount of data to connect. One idea that emerged was to write fuel levels on a card for display in the co-pilot's window as the plane taxied to the stand. This meant the refuelling crew didn't have to wait for communication to be made with the busy cockpit and could go to work much faster. Another idea was to move the fuel truck 5 metres forward from its usual position so the baggage handlers could start to unload earlier.

This and several other initiatives created by the easyJet crew meant that turnaround time was reduced from 40 minutes to 25 minutes, which has been maintained ever since. This reduction has allowed an extra flight to be squeezed in every day, which in turn has had a dramatic impact on financial performance and reputation.

It's incredible how much duplication or missed opportunities exist because people work in silos. Very often the answer has been researched and developed in another department – right under our nose. Some organisations are stealing the tech start-up concept of hackathons. They're locking their staff (not literally) in a room for 48 hours. They have all the research that's ever been done and a constant supply of pizzas. These events work well if they are cross-departmental, each brings their research for another department to read. Seeing what the adjacent silo is working on always throws up opportunities.

Be Bold

'A good breakfast sets you up for the day' went the challenge from our client, a traditional English baker and bread supplier to supermarkets throughout the UK. The problem was that breakfast seemed to be going out of fashion and sales of bread were dwindling. Our client's understanding of how families consumed bread was restricted to either their own experience or to 'focus groups'. Knowing that in research people tend to either forget or fantasise about the reality of their true behaviour, we asked our clients – a bunch of middle-aged men – to get up early and spend breakfast with a family. Each director would adopt a family and have Monday, Tuesday, Saturday and Sunday breakfast with them. Clearly they had to fit around the families' schedules, even if that meant getting up very early.

Initially the directors were keen, but as the sessions approached they all cancelled, one by one. They seemed uncomfortable about spending this much time out of the office and in such an unusual, uncontrolled environment. Undeterred we rearranged and in some cases re-rearranged. There comes a point when you have to put your foot down.

Finally we had a full house, and eight directors got up early on Monday morning and set off. Later they admitted to us that they felt a little nervous about the breakfast experience. Maybe they were imagining housewives in negligees or husbands with hangovers? We met each director outside the house and accompanied them into the kitchen.

In all cases the scene that played out in front of us had Mum on fast forward while Dad was on pause. He was either standing up while eating, head in newspaper or tapping out an urgent email. While mum was busy on mute, the volume on the kids was turned up. The tension rose as the clock ticked, mum working all the time to feed the kids, pack the bags, remind about after-school activities and deal with the inevitable outbreak of sibling hostility. Finally the front door closed and peace descended.

The discomfort at the thought of the breakfast experience is long forgotten but the learning still lives with our clients several years on. What they saw was a game of brinkmanship in which Mum pushes the kids to eat breakfast and the kids wield their power to obstruct. They saw the impact of Dad opting out, and the relief felt by Mum as she completed the hardest task of the day – delivering her kids fed, on time and in the right mood to school. For the directors, perched slightly uncomfortably in the corner of the kitchen, this was a revelation. They recognised themselves as the upstanding, opted-out cereal eater.

It's impossible to innovate without experiencing discomfort. An innovator cannot be 'too posh to provoke'. People involved in the innovation process generally experience anything from mild discomfort to outright panic when they step outside the office to spend time with customers. One of our packaged goods clients was very nervous about the prospect. Faced with a choice between 'student house' and 'couple with two kids' he insisted he didn't want to do the student house – he was afraid they'd be punks or squatters. Imagine his relief when he arrived at his 'couple' house and was greeted by a shaven-headed, tattooed gentleman, a pit bull and a proudly displayed gun collection.

The lesson here is: Be bold. And remember, you will have paid customers to meet you, so get maximum value from the experience. You don't have to like them, and they don't have to like you.

Science and serendipity: Why getting out of the office could be worth a billion dollars

The development of new medicines is a highly regulated and high-investment activity. Once you've specified the performance criteria of a drug, it can take 10–15 years until it's launched. The costs are high and only a small percentage of development programmes actually make it to launch. This is why the patent protection that drug makers get is important to their business model, and is also one of the reasons counterfeiting is such an issue.

A major global pharmaceutical company client of ours had just had some bad news. Their antidepressant drug had failed its stage-two clinical trials, a development with potentially fatal implications for share price. But what did 'fail' actually mean? Digging into the target product profile (TPP) revealed very ambitious performance targets across key dimensions of efficacy, side effects and tolerability. To be successful this had to be a wonder drug. The research scientists had been stuck in the lab too long, mired in data and were struggling to connect with the raw emotions that patients, their carers and prescribers were actually experiencing.

So we hit the road, travelling across the US to meet people experiencing a wide range of depression. We met a musician whose guitars were covered with a thick layer of dust (he couldn't bear to touch them), a man who hadn't been outdoors for years and a painter who was hearing voices as we spoke to her. We met people who were young, people who were old, people who had care and people who had no one to turn to. As you might expect this experience was deeply moving, even for scientists who had studied depression for years. The face-to-face nature of our exploration was fundamentally different from that of reading reports. The data was the same, but the impact profoundly different.

What the scientists took away from their road trip was how crippling the side effects of antidepressants could be – something they had read about but not actually witnessed. One teenage sufferer had told them that full remission wasn't worth it if she gained 15 stone, stopped sleeping and sweated all day. The TPP demanded efficacy above all else, but patients seemed to be asking for a more balanced approach.

So the scientists went back to the lab and amended the TPP. Now they had rebalanced what they were looking for – slightly lower performance with less intrusive side effects, they found they already had the molecules to deliver against the TPP. The boldness of the road trip paid off. The scientists didn't have to start from scratch, slashing development time by several years – a development predicted to save the company over $1bn.

The Life Beyond

Human beings view their lives holistically; they don't distinguish excellence between different types of product or service. Think, for instance, about the intuitive way I can use iTunes to curate my music; anywhere, anytime I can reorganise and view my music collection. I get updates and downloads seamlessly. There's a real pleasure in curating the collection.

But only seconds after I download a new tune, a couple of letters come through my door. One is from my bank telling me about an unauthorised overdraft and the fee I have to pay for it. I can't remember what I've been spending and scrunch the letter into a tight ball. Then I notice another letter from the same bank asking me to take out a new type of credit card.

In that moment the contrast between the smooth, intuitive world of curating music and the impersonal world of understanding money is felt. This is how people see the world; today, what sets the standard in one market, sets the standard for all.

This is why we need to look beyond the market or category in which our products or services exist. We need better peripheral vision. What is setting the standards for our consumers – across a variety of markets, throughout their day or wherever they are?

Take the cocked-up bank communication example above. To understand a customer's life beyond bank communication might mean we observe several customers throughout a day (literally, we trail them) and log all their points of communication. We might observe that he or she:

* Received text message from a friend

* Had a phone call from Mum

* Read label on milk carton

- Read poster at bus top

- Listened to voicemail from colleague at work

As we build a long list, we might underline all the points of communication where we observed our customer smile, respond or frown. Each of these then needs more exploration. We might observe that the one-line text message from a friend in broken English with no punctuation or signoff elicits the biggest smile:

c u 8 cnr 2 n StMarks :)

(Translation: I'll see you at 8pm on the corner of Second Avenue and St Mark's Place. The smile will make sense to the recipient. Maybe it's a peace offering, maybe it's a promise, or maybe it's just the sender being friendly.)

This scrappy message is an interesting clue. It might be telling us that formal communication is less effective than short, sharp and friendly messages – something that could have huge implications for the bank. Later we'll collide this interesting clue with another and then another, and maybe we'll generate a powerful insight and idea.

Go to the Margins

Research budgets are limited, meaning that most research tends to focus on 'target markets'. (A dreadful phrase: we line a customer up in our sights and fire.) But inspiration for innovation is unlikely to come from 'normal consumers'. An innovator already has a mass of data on 'normal consumers' and his or her competitors are probably looking at the same data.

Innovation is fermented at the margins with the angry, the ambivalent, the rejecters and the 'do-it-yourselfers'. To some extent, provocation comes from getting inside the heads of the very people who have rejected you – or at least those who have an extreme or downright strange relationship with your brand or category.

Below is a digest of the weird and wonderful people we visited on three different projects. To find them was a creative process. First we developed a long list of people who had an eccentric or extreme relationship with our clients' product or service. Then, using all our contacts, we hit the phones and persuaded them to talk to us, or we went where they went and talked to them face to face. This type of activity takes guts and tenacity, some people are good at it and some people aren't. The financial investment in this type of 'stimulus' is always quite modest, but the provocation invaluable. Here are the three projects with a selection of the people we met up with:

Innovation is fermented at the margins with the angry, the ambivalent, the rejecters and the 'do-it-yourselfers'

A pizza food chain looking to break into the breakfast 'day-part'

- Several large early-rising labourers, regular patrons of a local 'greasy spoon'

- School kids whose parents left for work before them, breakfast habits unknown

- Fast-food lover, but claimed to eat a balanced diet by never eating until the evening

- Hale and hearty breakfast advocate, vociferous fast food hater

- Anti-capitalist, anti-fast food, vegetarian class-war activist.

New banking 'pay for' advisory service

- Several small business owners who went bust through 'lack of good advice' (they were angry)

- The wives and husbands of badly advised small business owners (they were even more angry)

- Informal and possibly illegal providers of microloans to various immigrant communities

- Small-town accountants providing low-cost financial advice to their business clients.

A new anti-dandruff shampoo for men

- A bald man who bought large amounts of anti-dandruff shampoo

- A woman who claimed she left her boyfriend because of his dandruff

- The unfortunate boyfriend (interviewed in a separate location)

- Several men proud of never washing their hair, they claimed, due to cost

- Several herbal remedy doctors who claimed to be able to treat dandruff

- A mum who mixed a 'magic potion' anti-dandruff for her husband and neighbours.

Bet you're thinking that these projects look kind of fun? They are, but they need to be edgy. No point just talking to someone who likes you; it's much more provocative to meet someone who really hates you, who rejects you or uses your product or service in a way you'd never intended. Although it may be unpleasant listening to these views, within them are the seeds of something useful. I'm not saying that you need to wear a bulletproof vest to innovate, but you do need to step outside your comfort zone.

The Many Lenses of Provocation

So far we've picked up clues about how our customers see things beyond our market, segment or category. We've gathered clues from people with extreme or eccentric relationships with our product or service. So the lens of provocation we've just peered through could be termed the customer or consumer lens. But we've only just begun our quest. Now things are about to get really exciting. There are many other lenses of provocation beyond the customer lens and we need to gather more clues through them.

One lens or provocation we often look through is the 'capability lens' – the skills and capabilities the organisation possesses. Think of this as 'supply side' creativity. Before we got the bakery company we previously encountered to hang out with their customers over breakfast we asked them to describe the skills and capabilities of their business. Their list was uninspiring:

- We're a lowest-cost operation

- We deliver nationwide

- We've got a best-in-class logistics division

- Expert seasonal produce buyer

- Short-order specialist regional bread producer.

Our aim was to get the executives to reframe their organisation's capabilities so that they might 'see' their business in a new way. So we asked the bakery's executives to re-express their capabilities. To make it easier for them, we asked that they imagine they were addressing a 5-year-old. The list that came back was very different:

- When you sleep, we work

- We have big ovens that can cook practically anything

- We love bread

- We know more about bread than just about anyone

- We're publishers, not just bakers (we have the most bread recipes on our website).

This exercise surprised even the bakery executives. Suddenly a world of 'new business' ideas opened up: 'Maybe we could joint venture our distribution with other businesses that work at night, such as newspapers? Maybe we should start a cookery skills campaign to teach the lost art of bread making?' Many more ideas tumbled out once they reframed 'who' they were.

A clever trick on the quest to provocation is to ask of your organisation: 'What if what is true about ourselves is false?' This sentence is quite a mouthful, but it's so useful I'm going to repeat it: 'What if what is true about ourselves is false?' This is provocation on steroids. Many of the world's greatest innovations have come from contrarians: 'What if we could fly? What if we could go to the moon? What if we could offer holidays in space?'

Just to illustrate the point let's take a simple product like shampoo: How do you break the rules?

Rule	What if ...
Liquid	We were solid, maybe a sculpted bar?
Use in shower	We were a pre-treatment for dry hair?
Cleans	We add gunk?
Morning	We were used before bedtime?
Sold in shops	We were made at home?

The broken rules are often illuminating. Each is a starting point for creative exploration. I'll bet you're quite surprised at how much potential my rule-breakers have? In the spirit of serendipitous discovery, grab a paper and pen and write down the rules in your industry. How would you break each one?

A comforting axiom of innovation is that very few challenges are genuinely new. There will likely be someone or something who has tackled a challenge related to yours. At ?What If! we call this a 'Related World' and finding them is an essential key to innovation.

Related natural worlds have long been a source of serendipitous invention:

- **Velcro:** After a day of hunting in the French Jura Mountains in 1941, George de Mestral inspected the burrs in his woollen clothes and his dog's coat. He found hundreds of little hooks engaging the loops in the material and fur. This natural hook and catch system gave him the initial idea for Velcro. De Mestral went on to make a machine to duplicate hooks and loops out of nylon.

- **Roll-on:** In the late 1940s, Helen Barnett Diserens joined US deodorant producer MUM. Inspired by what was then a new invention, the ballpoint pen, she developed an underarm deodorant based on the same idea. The product we now all know went on sale in the mid 1950s, marketed as Ban Roll-On.

- **Bullet Train:** Japan's bullet train was the fastest train in the world but every time it exited a tunnel the changed air pressure produced a worryingly loud bang. The solution was found by studying the kingfisher, which dives into water with little splashing. The front end of the train was redesigned to mimic the beak of this creature. Not only did the bang go away, but the train's fuel consumption improved as well.

Looking to a Related World for provocation takes guts in a large organisation. It's an unconventional thing to do, but the pay-off can be spectacular as BP found out.

In 2007, US gasoline prices reached new highs and drivers were starting to use smartphone apps to find the lowest prices in town. Increasingly gas was seen as a commodity: 'gas is just gas' as customers put it. BP had begun asking itself a fundamental question: 'What's the future of premium-grade petrol in an increasingly price-driven market?'

BP's global fuels technology team began work to create the right base molecule which, when added to BP gasoline, had a cleaning effect on a car's fuel system and helped restore it to its previous state. Launched as 'Invigorate' in 2008 across the mid-West and east Gulf Coast, the additive helped cars run 'younger for longer'. Success was almost immediate; Invigorate outperformed the rest of the industry by 2% and consumer perceptions of value for money and quality increased significantly. This was all the more remarkable given the backdrop of such a tough economy.

Key to this innovation project, known as 'The Living Car', was an exploration of Related Worlds. The quest for provocation had led the BP and ?What If! team to spend a lot of time riding in cars. We had observed how many drivers related to their car, not as 'hardware' but almost as a living thing. They would pat the dashboard, talk to the car in appreciative terms and make excuses for malfunctioning items. Those who viewed their car as a pet, or even an extension of the family were not interested in how the car worked. The engine and the gasoline that powered it just weren't that interesting to the drivers, much in the same way that the inner functioning of the human body was uninteresting to them. 'Sure, I got a liver. How does it work? Don't know.'

This led the innovation team to track down experts who had related issues. One such person was a herbal doctor. They recounted how they 'sold' remedies that rejuvenated different organs. They shared the 'softer' herbal language they used to describe their products. This led the team to develop the idea of a gas that enabled your car to stay younger for longer and enjoy the vibrancy of youth. What car (pet) owner could resist that?

BP launched Invigorate across 10,000 gas stations in the US. Instead of launching with their premium grade fuel only, Invigorate was made available across all three grades. Even people with rusty old bangers and who don't normally buy premium fuel love their cars. The financial impact of Invigorate is millions of dollars.

As the story illustrates, the quest for provocation can take us to some interesting and unexpected places. But the barrier to a Related Worlds exercise is often within ourselves: 'What will people think of me? Will my colleagues realise what I'm trying to do?' Carefully choose a few Related Worlds exercises and explain why you have picked them. In the story above when I mentioned 'herbal doctor' I bet you raised your eyebrows? That's the reaction a Related Worlds exercise often gets. But when I mentioned the scale of the payoff, I'm guessing it all made sense.

Some other ways to provoke new insights are:

Looking out into cyberspace where people are having conversations about the topics they care about can be a great source of challenge and inspiration. Special interest sites and blogs are an established part of the provocation armoury. There are specialist websites for everything from breast cancer to bankruptcy to left-handed golfers. To be able to get involved in the kind of informal and unfettered dialogue that these sites have is very revealing. Somehow people really let themselves go in cyberspace. They spew out their feelings, full of passion, with minimal editing and few revisions. Brilliant! For an innovator it feels easier interjecting with online discussion groups – the anonymity of it all means you can provoke and push in a way you probably wouldn't do face to face.

Mapping the flow of cash and profit in your broader market – suppliers, customers and influencers – can be a great source of provocation as well. Where are the best margins? Where is all the growth? Where is all the intellectual property? Where are salaries higher? Who gets all the glory? Stand back and allow yourself to inhabit the skin of others in this 'value map'. This will surely prompt you to throw out some clues. Some of the bravest innovators are unafraid to explore above and below themselves in the value chain. IBM has been very successful in morphing from making weighing machines to mainframe computers to laptops to consultancy.

Organise your smartphone using randomised tools such as Flipboard, Pinterest and StumbleUpon. Flick through the pages and allow yourself to get lost in one of these apps. It's the modern-day equivalent of walking around a library and picking up a book to read at random. This is where serendipity can really kick in. You can connect two seemingly unconnected pages or connect your challenge with a page selected at random.

The Prepared Mind

When Pasteur said 'In the field of observation, chance only favours the prepared mind' he meant that we've got to do our homework. We need to prepare ourselves so that we can really see things and hear things for the first time.

So first we've got to tune our antennae. Executives, understandably, find it hard to switch from head-down operational mode to open-minded customer observation mode. It's important to tune your antennae out of 'opinionated' frequency and into 'no preconception' frequency. I like the description of this as 'looking with soft eyes'. I've stolen this from an episode of HBO's hit series *The Wire*. Episode Two, Series Four is a must-see for all about to embark on the quest for provocation. The detective stands back and allows the facts to wash over her. She doesn't dive in with preconceptions. This gives her the ability to see what all the other bullheaded detectives can't. In the end she gets the bad guy.

There's an antennae tuning exercise we invented at ?What If! called 'Consumer Shoes'. It works for an innovation team, sponsor team or a wider group of stakeholders. Here's how it worked with the directors of a global confectionary company:

> **When Pasteur said 'In the field of observation, chance only favours the prepared mind' he meant that we've got to do our homework**

I started by sitting the guys (yes, all men) in a circle facing me and got the usual jokes about how this felt 'like an AA meeting'. Then I gave them unpopular news: 'Today you are going to role-play customers'. I explained that we were going to focus on a key segment; teenage females. I then gave the director to my left an identity. I told him: 'You are Phoebe and you're 18 years old'. The next director was Samantha, 17 years old, then Jane, then Jill – you get the picture. The mutiny started when I asked them to respond to my questions in the first person and in character. We have better things to do they insisted, but I held my ground and the directors were soon enjoying themselves.

I started with general questions about customers' lives:

* Who do you fancy?

* What haven't you told your mum about your life?

- How much money do you have in your purse?

- What are you most afraid of?

- How would you describe a typical night out with your friends?

These were great questions to get my roleplayers in the mood and thinking like their alter ego. Then I ask questions that are about the market or category, in this case it was confectionary, or more broadly treats. So:

- How many sweets/much candy do you buy?

- How would you feel if you could never buy sweets again?

- When do you eat confectionary and where are you when you're eating it?

The final group of questions is about the brand:

- What sort of person makes this brand?

- What other brands does someone who buys this brand buy?

- What three words would you use to describe this brand?

Over the course of an hour the directors tried hard to answer my questions as if they were their consumers. There was a lot of laughter but quickly they realised this was a serious exercise. It's the commercial equivalent of asking a politician how much a pint of milk costs. Finally, I released them from the exercise and asked them how they thought they performed. They felt they had done well on pricing and distribution questions but not so well on general 'day in the life' type questions.

But the Consumer Shoes exercise had only just begun. Having asked the directors to move to a circle of chairs in the outside of the room I opened a side door and in walked the real Phoebe, Samantha, Jane, Jill and the rest of them. The room was silent as my executives realised what was about to happen. I sat the girls down in the same places as their male alter egos had been sitting and asked exactly the same questions in exactly the same order. You could have heard a pin drop. The answers of course from the 'real' customers are not representative of all customers, but nonetheless it was fascinating to contrast the two sets of answers.

Some of the directors were much better than others at understanding their consumers. Some clearly hadn't a clue. Some directors had accurately predicted what a typical night out with friends was like and could also paraphrase how they would feel if the brand was discontinued. Other directors really struggled with the night out – they didn't know where their customers would go, what they might eat or drink or what type of conversations they would have. They also predicted the customers' world would fall apart if the brand was discontinued, something that wasn't true.

Until an innovation team or their sponsors recognise their expertise, biases or knowledge gaps, they will find it hard to listen openly to others

This is not an exercise in humiliation, but rather one that seeks to illuminate who in the group has genuine insight, and who is biased towards one point of view. Clearly the game is dynamite if mishandled, but in all cases I have found it immensely powerful. Since we invented this exercise I think we have run it over a thousand times and all over the world. Until an innovation team or their sponsors recognise their expertise, biases or knowledge gaps, they will find it hard to listen openly to others. Either they will not pick up clues because they think they know it all and keep reverting to a pet theory (a theory someone never lets go of, which reappears year after year), or they may actually fear they know nothing and overcompensate with too many opinions.

The exercise is particularly good for confident veteran executives who 'have seen it all before'. These guys can be a pain in the innovation butt. The Consumer Shoes exercise enables them to realise just how much the world has moved on. Plus it's very convenient as the exercise can take place in the office.

So now we're totally tuned up. The quest for provocation can begin. But where shall we look first? After 20 years of 'preparing minds' to find provocation, there are places I'd always try first.

Great clues are found when people are forced to DIY. Recently I came into work in a taxi and took this picture of the driver. This guy was addicted to his screens and he's providing us with a big clue. Clearly the auto manufacturer isn't giving him what he needs and he's had to make it up himself. When people develop their own solutions then they are giving you a big fat clue.

When people develop their own solutions then they are giving you a big fat clue

Another hot hunting ground for clues is when you spot a 'contradiction'. We once partnered with a global bank looking at innovative new ways to deliver better service. We visited a whole range of loyal and lapsed customers. We visited them in their homes and asked to talk in the place where they made most financial decisions. We squeezed into home offices, kitchens and even bedrooms. We heard most customers tell us how important money was to them, how they counted their pennies and how essential it was to have the same attention to detail in a bank. In fact these consumers were very critical of the bank's attention to detail. But when we asked them to open up their desks, their account book or online files we saw something surprising. In fact we saw very little at all. Most customers had no idea what financial products they had, what rates they were charged or how healthy their financial performance was. It was an extraordinary contradiction and, again, a big fat clue.

A final point on 'preparing to see' is to not be afraid to let things get a little messy. It's amazing the things you observe when people shrug off social convention and reveal the raw emotion underneath. The issue is that many people won't tell you what they really think about your product or service. Maybe because your product, the product you love, is pretty boring to them. Or maybe it feels too painful to talk about some issues, for instance the overweight talking about cholesterol or smokers talking about smoking. Sometimes the subject matter is just plain embarrassing – like erectile dysfunction, body odour, haemorrhoids, bankruptcy or illiteracy. Sometimes we need to give these people a little nudge to get them talking.

We once explored how recently divorced men and women managed their finances post split-up. To spice up the dialogue we organised two rows of chairs facing each other. In trooped five recently divorced men and five recently divorced women. We asked them to sit opposite each other. Within a few minutes the two sides of the room were getting very heated with each other. One woman admitted that she'd known from 'the day I walked down the aisle' that the marriage wouldn't last. Many of her fellow females agreed and this sent the men into a spiralling series of intimate counter-claims. Before chairs were thrown, we halted the session. It had been extremely rich in clues for the financial services company – none of which conventional research had uncovered.

Another way to nudge people into talking is to use humour. Before the US launch of Unilever's brand Axe's, Axe Brand Director Neil Munn and ten of his team spent a day in a comedy club in Chicago. They were joined by sixty 18-year-olds. The lights dimmed and, on stage, comedians cracked gags all about the dating and mating game. The first comedian told a story about how a young guy approached a group of women intent on pulling. The audience laughed and squirmed with embarrassment as his pathetic lines were brutally dissected by the female pack. After the laughter died down, the house lights came up and Munn led an analysis with the audience about why this was so funny. The clues flowed: 'We learnt more that day than we'd ever done', says Munn, 'the levity and shared experience allowed those guys to open up about their emotions, their vulnerability, like nothing else.'

Paradoxically, another way to shrug off convention is to create a sense of normality. Once we held a clue-gathering session with psoriasis sufferers in a swimming pool. We were all in our swimming costumes, all the same – you can imagine how much easier it was for people to compare conditions and speak openly in a place they usually avoid.

In the same vein we undertook a project called 'The Future of Sex' for a condom manufacturer. Before the project started, our team and the client's team met to 'normalise' together. This involved us meeting and talking about sex, using as many sexual words and definitions as we'd ever heard of. We carried on until words and concepts that were normally taboo were easy to say. Without this process we couldn't have talked openly with each other.

"

Significant inventions are not mere accidents. The erroneous view (that they are) is widely held, and it is one that the scientific and technical community, unfortunately, has done little to dispel. Happenstance usually plays a part, to be sure, but there is much more to invention than the popular notion of a bolt out of the blue. Knowledge in depth and in breadth are virtual prerequisites. Unless the mind is thoroughly charged beforehand, the proverbial spark of genius, if it should manifest itself, probably will find nothing to ignite.

Nobel laureate Paul Flory, upon the occasion of receiving the Priestley Medal, the highest honour given by the American Chemical Society. *Serendipity, Accidental Discoveries in Science.* Royston M. Roberts

Provoked. What Next?

Think of a detective movie. The crime scene is where we gather clues. Back at the station detectives are gathered in the incident room. The walls are covered with clues; it looks a confusing mess and the detectives stand back, stroking their chins, trying to spot a pattern.

Innovators everywhere follow an equivalent procedure. We're looking at the facts, the clues, and we're thinking to ourselves 'Why is that?' At the same time we're looking across clues garnered from all our lenses of provocation. Within this bubbling mental soup connections are made and hunches are formed.

We call these hunches 'insights'. An insight is an important concept to innovators. It gives us a deep understanding of why people do what they do – so penetrating is a good insight that it naturally generates potential solutions. A good insight is like a well-fertilised garden – it can't help but generate ideas. The converse is true. A lack of insights is like a desert, only weak ideas will grow here.

For the sake of tidiness I'll conclude our detective metaphor; the 'arrest' is the insight that drives an idea and the 'conviction' is a successful launch.

To make the clues to the insight process real, let's say we're exploring ways to improve the consultation a patient will have with a doctor. Some of clues we have are:

- I heard several doctors say that if they had more time to explain how to take medicine regularly most patients would recover sooner

- I saw the doctor's receptionist try to help a patient with the location of the pharmacy

- I read the regulations that permit a lower standard of training for minor medical interventions such as the taking of blood and administering of some medicine

- I read about patients who are using websites to self-prescribe

- I heard about people who share their medicines so their friends don't have to bother going to the doctor

- I saw some doctors rushing through the consultation

- I saw some patients not really understand what the doctor was saying

- I read that 40% of patients have nothing wrong with them that rest and a balanced diet couldn't sort out

- I saw patients sit in the waiting room for 2 hours

- I heard a patient say she felt like a sheep being shoved in and out of a pen

- I read that you can pay £65 to have a doctor visit you.

Note that these clues are observations, they may not be representative but they are clean objective observations. They are a mix of observations about how people behaved, what people said, what things cost and how things work. A clue always starts with 'I heard ...' or 'I saw ...'

or 'I read ...' This is an easy way to remember the difference between a clue and an insight. Also note that the list above is a rich mix of clues derived from looking through many lenses of provocation. This is where serendipity happens – it's the mixing of lenses of provocation that counts.

Some of these clues could connect to make the following insights:

1. Both doctors and patients believe the consultation process isn't working.

2. A 7-minute consultation has a diagnosis stage and an advice stage. The diagnosis needs the doctor but the advice is a lower grade activity.

3. Patients are expecting to have a bad experience. They're in a bad mood before the consultation has begun.

4. While some non-skilled medical staff have little to do, the doctors are rushed off their feet.

Insights can be inspirational or they can be mediocre. Insights 1 and 3 above are dull but insight 2 is very exciting. A good insight propels you to have novel solutions. In this case I'm immediately thinking of ideas. Maybe a more highly trained receptionist could handle part of the 'advice' stage. Maybe doctor surgeries could have an incoming receptionist and a dispatch type receptionist? The dispatch receptionist could make sure patients aren't leaving the surgery with any unresolved issues, or take their time with confused patients and explain how to take their medicine? Or maybe I'll combine insights 2 and 4. Now I'm thinking that after the doctor has seen the pathology report, the same receptionist can call the non-critical cases with the test result.

Let's Get Practical

In this chapter we've explored how some organisations force themselves out of a dangerous thinking 'rut'. A quest for provocation might take a few weeks to set up, a month or two to execute and a couple of weeks to extract the gold. Your checklist might look something like this:

Preparation

* Before you do anything check first the answer isn't hiding under your nose. You could save yourself a lot of time and money.

* Look each other in the eye and recognise that the quest takes courage. If it's not hurting, it's not working – corny but true.

* Tune your antennae. I showed you how a Consumer Shoes exercise allows you to do this as a team. Without recognising the biases we all have, or the lack of understanding some of us have, the innovation team will quickly become dysfunctional.

The quest

There are many lenses of provocation. The trick is to look through several but only extract observations or 'clues' ('I heard, I saw, I read …') at this stage.

The main lenses are:

* Consumer: get inside their heads, beyond your market, sector or category. Find extreme and eccentric users.

* Capability: look at what you're good at with fresh eyes.

* Related Worlds: who else has cracked this challenge?

Extracting the gold

Get in the Incident Room and look across the hundreds of clues you've gathered. Collide them together to create new insight. This is the foundation of ideas and innovation.

3

Making Ideas Real

The Innovator's Favourite Weapon

In 30 seconds

If you only had 30 seconds I'd tell you:

'Making Ideas Real' is a state of mind that drives us to translate an idea into a form that we can react to immediately and emotionally.

◆

'Making Ideas Real' delivers much better innovation because it forces us to stop talking and start doing.

◆

'Making Ideas Real' is the practical way to 'tolerate risk'.

◆

'Making Ideas Real' is suitable for all organisations in all markets.

◆

You can make things real at every stage of the innovation process; early stage conversations, simulations, prototypes, pilots and even beyond launch.

◆

At the heart of 'making it real' is an iterative approach – a programme of experiments that test and build on each other.

◆

There are four pillars to making things real: a good enough mindset, low-cost approach, stealth and the behaviour of 'greenhousing'.

The Boots name has been on UK high streets for over 160 years. Today, Boots UK has close to 2500 stores across the UK, many of which were previously branded 'Boots the Chemists'. Over the years, it has continued to dispense pharmaceutical products to the nation, with pharmacists fulfilling doctors' prescriptions 'over the counter'. However, this high street veteran is no stranger to cutting-edge innovation techniques.

?What If! was charged by Boots UK to break the autopilot buying habits associated with pharmacy shopping. Research showed that time-pressed shoppers didn't like to bother the pharmacist with questions and would go to nearby shelves where less powerful drugs were sold and pick up the same cough remedy or gastric bug buster they always used, regardless of whether it was the right one for them. Working with the shop-floor employees in one of Boots 'category A' branches, we had complete freedom to move products around, put new packs on shelves and change the signage.

When the ?What If! crew arrived on a Sunday night, we had a few hunches about how we could direct shoppers to ask the pharmacist for advice, but at this stage we deliberately hadn't worked these into finished ideas.

Working in shifts over the next 12 hours, we reorganised the store in and around the pharmacy area. The store manager drafted her family and friends to lend a hand. By 8am, that section of the store had several subtle changes, including new signs on the shelves telling customers to ask the pharmacist for advice and new scripts for the staff to use.

The doors opened for business and we stood back to observe shopper behaviour. We had trained the staff to help question shoppers but it was clear that our overnight changes were more confusing than helpful. Customers clearly weren't interested in our signs. In the quiet spell after lunch we increased the size of the signage – having two graphic artists with us meant there was no end to the alterations we could make.

After a full day of observing, questioning and reorganising the store we retired to a local coffee shop to reflect on Day One. Overnight, the relief team continued the process of adapting the store, but it was clear that our proposed reorganisation of the store wasn't working. Our hunches just weren't clicking. So we changed tack and created peel-off notes telling customers to ask the pharmacist's advice. We stuck them to the backs of hundreds of headache, cough and cold medicine packs located on the store's shelves.

By the end of Day Two some customers were reading our peel-off notes, but not enough to make a difference. That evening the team was starting to feel uncomfortable; we had used half our time and had little to show for it. Later, one team member would describe this week as a journey 'from the depths of despair to the heights of joy'.

One of our 'experimenters' pushed the peel-off label further. We removed all our signs and labels (effectively the last 48 hours' work). Then we took the 'prescription only' drugs from behind the counter, emptied the pills and powders, and put the empty packs on the shelf with increased signage recommending these as the superstrength 'best' products – as prescribed by the pharmacists.

It was clear we had hit on a good idea. On Wednesday, shoppers paused, read the label and started thinking about what headache product was best for them. That day many of the 'empty' superpower packs were sold (exchanged for full ones by the pharmacist). Boots UK employees were having to restock the shelves very rapidly. Simon Potts, a senior leader within Boots UK, was delighted. He quietly extended the idea to eight more stores. The evidence was now overwhelming; on average a considerable sales uplift in the pharmacy area and all for very little on-cost. Within a few weeks the idea spread to all stores nationally.

For many years, Boots UK had analysed the status of pharmaceutical sales, but what eventually changed wasn't due to data analysis, it was due to an experimental 'make it real' approach.

The ability to extract the killer points from a mass of data, or to deliver the 'elevator pitch' have become the staple diet for any ambitious person in a large company (after years of practice they're hardwired into most senior executives). The more life at work revolves around 100-page presentations, the more distant we feel from customers. I've noticed many executives refer to 'the real word', or 'the outside world'. Sounds to me like a tacit acknowledgement that their world is genuinely unreal.

'Making Ideas Real' is a state of mind that constantly provokes us to translate an idea into a form which customers would recognise. It means that we come close to the uninhibited and unconscious reactions that consumers have. Making things real effectively displaces a business dialogue (which can externalise consumers as 'they') with a first person dialogue. Now it's more about 'my' reactions, my gut feel and my judgement.

Making ideas real is for every type of organisation. Service organisations that deal with intangible products, online businesses, business to business organisations and consumer goods companies can all make things real.

Making ideas real plays a critical role at every stage of the innovation lifecycle. Early on, when we're just kicking around half-formed thoughts, 'making it real' means we change the way we talk to each other. Now we've stopped describing the idea using 'business-speak' and more as a customer or consumer would see it and speak about it. Co-creating ideas with consumers at these early stages speeds innovation.

Later on we can make a product idea real through a rough sketch, or make a service idea real through simple play-acting. Making preliminary ideas into basic prototypes enables quick feedback and builds the confidence of the development team. Now you can iterate the idea and get yet more feedback from a wider community. Making the business model real allows colleagues from across the enterprise to contribute and gives it a fighting chance during the inevitable compromises commercialisation brings. And it doesn't stop on launch day. Many organisations are seeing this as just one stage of the innovation process with further development loops planned in soon after launch.

This chapter explores how to make things real along the development cycle of an idea, and shares some observations on what it takes to carry a 'Make Ideas Real' mindset with you at all times.

Make It Real: **At the Birth of an Idea**

Realness is useful from the very first moment an idea is born, way before the design and development stage. Say you are having a conversation with a colleague at the bar, in a taxi or over the phone. Your colleague has the seed of an idea: You can suck your teeth and raise your eyebrows. You can interrogate the idea (What revenue will it make? What return on investment will it deliver?) or you can suggest that together, here and now, you make it real.

Making things real gives us the opportunity to change the script and fundamentally improve the chances of innovation. So let's make it real: Who can we imagine using it? What would they say to a friend about it? Does it fit in my pocket?

> *'OK, I'm not sure I get your idea yet, but let's sit down and explore for a while - how can we make it real now? Can you draw it for me? And let's get Saskia to join us; she's the customer, not us.'*

> *'Hey, this new product idea sounds kind of interesting, but how real can we make it now? Let's call up a friendly buyer and pretend it exists - let's see if we can get a meeting.'*

> *'OK, I'm curious about this new service idea. Let's act it out now: You be the buyer and I'll be the seller. What are we going to say and do?'*

'How real can we make it now?' This is one of the greatest innovation questions ever. It encourages us to dig deeper into the customer experience. Realness is a fabulous early stage activity. It can be a conversation, a simulation or a basic mock-up.

Dave explaining the football offside trap to me using tabletop items.
There is no end to the value of making things real!

Make It Real: **Co-Creation Makes Momentum**

Listen to this. It's a radio advertisement for 48, a new mobile phone operator launched in 2012 that's taking the Irish market by storm:

'I will flirt, kiss, date and dump. I'll even break your heart. I'll give guys my number knowing it's a digit short. I'll go out for an hour and sneak in the next morning. I will wake up on your couch and haven't a clue who you are. And if you don't like it, go fu** yourself'.

If you winced reading that then it's probably because you're not the intended audience. 48, owned by Telefonica, is aimed at 18 to 22 year olds in Ireland. Its unique pricing structure and gritty advertising has been a massive hit.

❝

> *Rather than deploy a traditional sequential approach, they set about finding supercreative teens to work with, throwing them together for a short space of time*

Having decided to target a youth audience, Telefonica soon recognised that no matter how much their middle-aged executives hung out with teens, they'd never be able to accurately reflect their approach to life, their humour and their language.

So Telefonica did something radical. Rather than deploy a traditional sequential approach where executives commission research and then develop ideas with an external agency, they set about finding supercreative teens to work with, throwing them together for a short space of time and aiming for a product with breakthrough relevance to the target market.

The recruitment of the creative teens took longer than they thought. They were looking for 18 to 22 year olds who were smart, cool and engaged with life. They also had to have a creative skill like copywriting, film-making or acting. Above all, these guys had to be able to work together in a room for a week. It took many weeks of interviews to find just the right characters. The brief given to the creative teens was to create a shockwave of an idea that would surge across Ireland and grab market share fast – 18 to 22 year olds must love it (and their parents most likely would hate it).

The newly recruited creative team spent a week of organised chaos in their own space in Dublin. There was a skeleton plan, a couple of skilled facilitators acting as ringmasters, lots of wall space to put ideas up, lots of music, lots of laughter and lots of coffee. Ideas for every aspect of the new concepts were tossed around: communication ideas, name ideas, media strategy ideas, pricing structure ideas, call centre script ideas and distribution ideas were drawn, acted out, written down. Within minutes they were re-drawn, re-acted and re-written.

The Telefonica team was lean and, where possible, close to the target age group. Older and more senior members of the team popped in every now and then, but mindful of their veteran vibe potentially infecting the group they quickly disappeared. The room gradually filled up with creative content. By Friday there was no need for a presentation, the big idea was writ large on the walls: 'Turn 18 – the best 48 months of your life lie ahead of you'. Within a week the entire marketing mix had been made real.

But the co-creation and momentum didn't just stop after the initial week of brand development. Telefonica hired some of the participants to act as creative guardians of the brand. They were given two weeks to write TV scripts, radio ads and outdoor communications that would strike a chord with their peers (fellow 18 to 22 year olds).

> 66
>
> *This was a fast and low cost process of co-creation and the iteration didn't stop at launch*

Within weeks a TV advert was shot, a radio advert recorded and 48 was launched with a unique offer only available to 18 to 22 year olds – all texts, all calls to all networks for €10 a month. There was no traditional brand or operational thinking, just engagement with a carefully selected group of customers. This was a fast and low cost process of co-creation and the iteration didn't stop at launch; Telefonica reckoned they had 48 about 70% right at launch; they knew that 48 could and would evolve after launch as consumers interacted with it.

This is virtuoso level 'making it real'. Six months after launch 48 has almost 100% awareness amongst the target audience and is the fastest growing network in Ireland. The project took four months, from a completely blank sheet to launch. A more traditional approach might have looked like this:

Sponsor team agree objectives, governance process and appoint project team

Team forms and commissions research

Review research and develop brief for communication and product development

Generate and review new ideas

Agree a route forward

Early stage research and concept refinement

Engage stakeholders, develop business case

Test business case and further socialise with more stakeholders

Go/No go meeting

Plan for launch

This sequential process would have taken at least 12 months with no guarantee that the quality of the output would have been any better than the unconventional co-creation route.

The development of 48 (don't go to YouTube and check out the advertising if you have an 18-year-old daughter) is a great co-creation story. Rather than commission research, Telefonica put all their effort into finding the right co-creators and then gave them the right environment with a clear brief.

Co-creation is the joint development of an idea with its ultimate users or operators. Telefonica got the ingredients right with 48 but don't be fooled; a week of creative chaos takes a lot of planning and skilful orchestration.

In my experience successful co-creation demands:

*   **A brief with limited scope:** Creativity loves constraints so don't burden your co-creators with endless blue-sky opportunities. The new 48 'brand' was tightly scoped. It was for a discrete age group and was to have a pricing structure below the nearest competitor.

*   **Handpicked customers:** Co-creation depends on the quality of the protagonists – don't skimp on this stage of the process. The big difference between the 48 approach and an open-source approach is the handpicked quality of the participants. The recruitment process took about three times as long as that of the co-creation period itself.

*   **Skeleton plan:** Co-creators need a ringmaster, someone who can get things back on track. The 48 co-creation week wasn't over-planned but it wasn't just random either.

♦ **A holistic approach:** Making things real like this enables you to iterate both execution and strategy in parallel. One minute the 48 team was working on the name and the distribution model the next.

♦ **Resources:** Co-creators need to be able to articulate their ideas in different mediums, but this doesn't have to cost the earth. The 48 team was deliberately limited to the ability to visualise ideas. This was all the group could cope with in the time allotted; anything more would have been a distraction.

♦ **Intensity:** A sense of urgency creates a frenetic and exciting atmosphere. On a practical note, the 48 co-creator customers were only available for a short time over the summer.

66

Don't be fooled. A week of creative chaos takes a lot of planning and skilful orchestration

Making it real isn't new

Over a hundred years ago Thomas Edison and his prototyping crew of 'Muckers' in Menlo Park, New York made thousands of experiments, pioneering electric lighting and many other inventions. I find it fascinating how his words from then are uncannily apt today. They read like a modern-day experimenters' instruction manual:

> *'If I find 10,000 ways something won't work, I haven't failed. I am not discouraged, because every wrong attempt discarded is often a step forward ...'*

> *'I never did anything worth doing entirely by accident ... Almost none of my inventions were derived in that manner. They were achieved by having trained myself to be analytical and to endure and tolerate hard work.'*

> *'Show me a thoroughly satisfied man and I will show you a failure.'*

> *'Just because something doesn't do what you planned it to do doesn't mean it's useless.'*

> *'Restlessness is discontent, and discontent is the first necessity of progress.'*

> *'Genius is 1% inspiration and 99% perspiration. Accordingly, a "genius" is often a talented person who has done his or her homework.'*

Make It Real: **Powering Prototypes and Validating Ideas**

Technology has had a huge impact on making things real. When I first started in the innovation business you'd have found us making prototypes out of cardboard and sticky-tape. Our office looked like a kindergarten at times. Today we can 'print' almost perfect 3D models in any part of the world. We can create functioning websites that simulate a new business overnight. And we can measure whether customers like our prototypes in many countries, simultaneously and in real time. This is a trend that will continue, but it's digitally enabled, not digitally led. You have to know the principles of making it real first.

Wrong thinking creates right results

Realness stories are the ripping yarns of the business world. The innovation story zigzags as unexpected outcomes block the path only for another opportunity to open up. These journeys of experimentation are real adventures – full of heartache, elation and heated conversations long into the night.

The development of Dyson's Dual Cyclone bagless vacuum cleaner is a terrific innovation adventure that saw James Dyson develop 5126 prototypes before he got it right. This is a story of constant experimentation and determination – Edison would have approved. But Dyson isn't just an inventor. His iterative approach helped him drive the initial idea to a test market, explore different sales channels and scale the business. Today Dyson's vacuum cleaners are the leading brand in many markets around the world. The experimental philosophy continues to pay off as further innovation hits the market; the Airblade hand drier worked, the contra-rotating washing machine didn't. James Dyson, now Sir James, is estimated to be worth a cool billion pounds.

The story starts in the late 1970s. Dyson was frustrated at how poorly his Hoover Junior was cleaning the house. A design student by training, he took the offending cleaner apart to reveal how the gradually thickening layer of dirt reduced suction and ultimately clogged the contraption.

'I was furious ... We were all victims of a gigantic con by the manufacturers. They fit these bags and the bloody things clog up immediately, and had done for 100 years. I had spent all this money on the most powerful vacuum cleaner ever produced, and it was essentially just as useless as the old one I had always had, which was permanently and irrecoverably clogged.'

Dyson had years earlier adapted the giant cyclonic dust extraction systems found in timber mills to suck away the excess spray paint from the manufacture of another invention of his – the Ballbarrow. With this in mind and still angry about the vacuum cleaner, he grabbed what was to hand in his kitchen at home: cereal boxes, kitchen scissors and sticky tape. Soon he'd built a fully functional foot-high cyclonic cone. When attached to the guts of the original vacuum cleaner, centrifugal force swirled the dirt upwards towards an exit hole but ultimately it collected in the base of the cone. Dyson cleaned the house twice to prove to himself that the thing actually worked.

There followed years of prototype development: 'My fingers numb with the chill, I huddled like Bob Cratchit over a single candle and prepared to hammer out another prototype cyclone ... For three years I did this alone ... sometimes I would lose control completely when a model went wrong after weeks of planning, and Jacob [his son] told me only recently how well he remembers the sound of sheets of acrylic shattering out in the coach house or down in the cellar and me exploding in a typhoon of vociferous profanity.' Eventually Dyson produced a bagless vacuum cleaner that could suck just about anything – including liquids – with no loss of suction.

There were many twists in the road to market for Dyson, but eventually he launched his first dual cyclonic vacuum cleaner in 1993 in the UK. The Dyson DC01 and its subsequent models marched across Europe, then Japan, Australasia and the US to become the best-selling vacuum cleaner everywhere. The market incumbents initially refused to believe the weird looking contraption built in a shed and twice the price of their cleaners was a threat. But eventually, when faced with plummeting shares, they responded with similar looking devices.

Dyson's approach to innovation is summed up in his phrase 'wrong thinking'. Innovation doesn't come out of carefully considered plans but thinking against the grain, making it real and knowing you'll have to go through many more iterations before it's right. 'Careful thinking' doesn't work because human beings have a great ability to self-censor, the fear of failure is so great that we block risky ideas – a kind of automatic safety response. When Dyson came up with the idea of the clear bin that collects the dust and detritus, everyone around him rubbished the idea. But Dyson believed in it. When he made it real, it became a big hit and now the clear bin is a much-copied feature.

Today Dyson insists that everyone who joins his company must assemble a Dyson Dual Cyclone cleaner on their first day at work. The wearing of ties is discouraged as they have no functional benefit. Design and engineering are one function. This is a business built on passion, tenacity and making ideas real as fast and as cheaply as possible.

Dyson went to amazing lengths to develop his idea, generating over 5000 prototypes. With each prototype he improved on the last. But in the back of his mind must have been the question 'Is this any good? Will anyone buy it?' If we share our prototypes or simulations widely, ask good questions and are prepared to 'hear' criticism, an experimental approach can help us validate an idea. Here are some simple but revealing questions an innovator has to ask:

* 'How would you sell this to a good friend?' Here we're listening for the exact language used to describe benefits. Customers can often articulate why something is so great, better than most executives or their advertising agencies.

* 'If you buy/use this, what do you stop doing?' This question digs at the real purpose of the new product or service. By forcing people to tell you what they'll drop to start using your fantastic new thing, you are really testing them. Remember that if it makes life more complex it isn't going to work.

* 'Is it better, the same or lesser value?' Don't ask this question as a leading question; give your respondent every opportunity to claim just parity value. If they do, its bad news. There is no reason for someone to change his or her purchasing habits for a parity value product or service.

Here are some lessons I've picked up over time for prototyping a product or simulating a service:

1. Plan for multiple rounds of experimentation – not just one long experiment.

2. Because this is an experiment you can afford to go against the grain. So don't self-censor. Let yourself go, and get radical.

3. Look each other in the eye and anticipate that not everything is going to work well. I like Facebook's motto: 'Move fast and break things'.

4. Start with several hypotheses, and resist the temptation to think you've got a winning idea early. The name of the game is to explore alternatives.

5. Recognise that you may need to kill your favourite prototype. Get over it. Don't get too attached; stay passionate but stay objective.

6. Start fast. Start quietly. Get your confidence up before you go public.

7. Start low cost and stripped down. You can always add more into the mix later.

8. Show your simulations or mock-ups early and frequently.

9. Be decisive in your adaptation. Testing ambiguous or weak features benefits no one. It's actually better to ramp up elements of your design to ensure a clear reading.

10. Be generous. Nothing is ever your idea. No one person will ever make it happen. Experimentation needs a community and a cooperative spirit.

Proof: Realness reduces risk

Realness is the practical answer to that most annoying management maxim: 'Tolerate failure'. Who the hell wants to tolerate failure when they have a family and a mortgage? Realness, on the other hand, is a more subtle and cultured concept. The fact that you conduct a series of micro experiments means you can push the emergency stop button much more easily than when speculating on the megascale launch.

An experimental approach to solving problems has also been proven to be more effective than a single burst of work. Researchers at Stanford University (Dow et al., 2009) asked 28 participants to work on a design to protect a raw egg in a fall. Half the participants designed, tested and iterated their egg protection ideas after 5, 10, 15 and 25 minutes. The other participants spent all their time on one design and were not allowed to test it until the end of the session. All had similar resources (paper, string and other materials). The results showed that the iterators significantly outperformed their non-iterating counterparts, achieving roughly double the non-breaking drop height – in some cases at 15 feet. Definitely one to try at home with the kids!

In this experiment the iterators said they felt stressed at first – under pressure to rush the experiment. But the report authors comment that it was this that drove them to discover flaws through iterating their designs, while the non-iterating participants were only able to speculate about their design's ultimate performance.

Make It Real: **Steel in Your Backbone**

Here's a simplified way of looking at an innovation journey:

$$I \times I \times I \times I = I$$

or

Identify × Insight × Idea × Impact = Innovation

In this equation:

◆ **Identify** = The strategic purpose

◆ **Insight** = An unmet need, opportunity for differentiation or whitespace

◆ **Idea** = The core concept

◆ **Impact** = Commercialising the idea through to launch.

You will note that this equation multiplies rather than sums. So if any element is a zero then the whole will sum to zero. In other words each stage of the innovation journey has a critical role to play.

No prizes for guessing that it's the last part of this journey that's most stressful, expensive and prone to screw-ups. Getting a new product or service over the line and into the market can be 99% of the task. It's not something for the faint-hearted, and many innovations fail because senior management either lose their nerve or lose touch with why the idea was so good in the first place. 'Making it Real' plays an important role in stiffening the resolve of both the innovation team and the sponsor team.

Metro, the free newspaper, is the morning diet of over 3.6 million UK commuters. But when it launched in 1999, it struggled to take off, despite its novelty of being smaller than most papers and stapled. The *Metro* leadership team in London decided to get out of the office and really get a taste of its market. They joined the newspaper delivery crews every morning at 5am. One morning they were standing at the mouth of the 'Drain'. This is London's Waterloo station escalator that disgorges hundreds of thousands of tired commuters every day. Looking at those commuters a realisation hit the *Metro* team. They were looking at prosperous office workers who normally didn't have a minute to spare, except when they were trapped commuting. These people in this moment were an advertisers' dream!

In the world of TV, some advertisement spots sell for a small fortune, during a break in the big game or a popular soap when there is a large captive audience. This is called Prime Time TV and *Metro*, buoyed by seeing all those bored, captive commuters cleverly adapted this phrase and called their advertising 'Prime Time Print'.

Now they needed to make it real for the Board of Directors and get their buy-in. This was important, as the *Metro* team were proposing a dramatic rise in advertising rates to match the Prime Time Print concept. The execs, inspired by what they had seen, persuaded the Board of Directors to leave the comfort of their boardroom and into the Drain. They too saw a great captive wave of bored commuters marching past. Seeing the customers for themselves, seeing that they lacked an easy-to-read London paper and seeing the sheer volume of them had a profound effect on the Board. They agreed to the change in rates.

A new business model was born; advertising rates and revenues went up. *Metro* is now the world's largest and most profitable free morning newspaper and has a thriving online presence. Today advertising rates are nearly double the average national newspaper rate and advertisers pay a premium to advertise in *Metro* to communicate with ABC1 adults and under 35s.

The *Metro* story demonstrates how the customer need and the sheer scale of the opportunity were made real. There is a big difference between talking about an opportunity in the boardroom and seeing or 'feeling' it for yourself. Making things real stiffened the resolve of the sponsor team and got innovation over the line.

Mock-ups can play clever tricks with your mind. Somehow picking up a mock-up and weighing it in your hands – it's as if it really existed. Then showing it to a customer and seeing their excitement – this can really change the chemistry in your brain. Suddenly you can't live without this new thing. Now you're committed to making it happen.

James Averdieck is the founder of Gü, an $80m chilled chocolate soufflés and brownies company operating in Germany, France, Australia, New Zealand and the UK. Their publicity heralds 'nibbles and naughties of chocolate extremism that's strictly for adults'. Hear James talk – 'Chocolate is about fun and indulgence; it brings out the kid in you and it reminds you of sticking your hand in the mixing bowl'. The Gü company rules are distinctive: 'Give in to happiness', 'Prudence is sooo 1658' and 'Ordinary is pointless'.

In 2002, when Averdieck had first thought of his upmarket chilled chocolate treats, he was going to call them 'The Belgian Chocolate Company'. He wasn't happy about the lacklustre brand name and hired a design company to come up with a brand identity. The design agency worked on the brief and asked him to come into their offices. He was shown a brand that the agency's creative director had found in Scandinavia. Called 'Gü', it had an exotic continental ring, it's onomatopoeic spelling was brilliant and the design looked perfect for the upmarket yummie-mummies that Averdieck was targetting. He was devastated; someone somewhere else had had his idea. Worse than that – they'd come up with a terrific name and packaging. Averdieck was heartbroken. But there was no brand in Scandinavia, there was no competitor. The agency had played a trick on Averdieck, the Gü identity was all his!

I think this is a superb example of mental trickery. Of course it's high stakes. Imagine how the meeting would have gone if Averdieck's reaction was: 'Ok, but we can do better yeah?' Creating a mock-up is not without risks. You are inviting criticism as well as praise. The point of this story is sometimes you only realise how much you want something when you realise you can no longer have it.

The sneaky but powerful realness trick was not lost on James. Weeks later he crept into upmarket Waitrose food store on London's Kings Road. Unobserved, he re-merchandised a small section of the store and carefully placed four empty mock-ups of his chocolate soufflé on the shelf. With baited breath he stood back. Within minutes a shopper approached, reached out and picked up one of the packs.

After what seemed like a lifetime she put the fake pack into her shopping basket. Averdieck then did two things. First he apologised to the shopper, whipped the soufflé out of her basket and fled. Second he made his mind up to devote himself to establishing Gü. This was the case for action that Averdieck needed – just enough proof to back up what he knew to be true, just enough to tip him over the edge and to convince him to take the next step on the journey.

Making It Real: **Before and After Launch**

Antony Jenkins, CEO of Barclays Retail and Business Bank, didn't need much convincing when the idea that became known as Barclays Pingit was presented to him in the summer of 2011. He knew that technology was going to change the world of finance forever and the time was right for the idea in front of him; sending small amounts of money from your smartphone to another phone. Instead of fiddling around with cash, people could now pay their babysitter, the corner shop or top up their offspring living away at college, all with a phone and all in seconds. With just a few clicks, the smartphone effectively instructs your bank to send money to another's bank – no cards, no ATM, no cash, no hassle.

'I love it, when can I have it? Can I have it by my wedding anniversary in October?' asked Jenkins of his team. The answer was a polite 'No'; the development programme would take at least two years. Jenkins refused to accept that a sequential process was necessary – he pushed for Christmas. Eventually they settled on a six-month development timetable and a Valentine's Day 2012 launch date.

An innovation whirlwind was unleashed. Instead of the typical programme management machine where activities are sequential, Barclays adopted a different approach. Now technologists, marketers, lawyers, risk teams and designers all had to work together in one large war room. They set up an iPhone development team in the UK in constant video contact with a mirrored BlackBerry and Android development team in Texas.

Barclays had previously launched a string of innovations including contactless payment cards, a credit card that doubled as a prepayment travel card (an 'Oyster Card' if you live in London) and payments from smartphones. This meant their intuition was good. They didn't research the idea, choosing instead to corral their colleagues into the war rooms and get their views on the day's work.

Within weeks of launch, Barclays Pingit had 500,000 downloads. Apple featured it as a best-selling app. Not bad for a bank in a traditionally sleepy sector that had become used to upstarts such as PayPal or Wonga nibbling at their lunch.

But this spirit of 'making it real' extended beyond the February launch. Rather than wait to get things perfect, Pingit kept iterating after launch. Within weeks the team realised they needed to drop the minimum age for Barclay's Pingit from 18 to 16 years. Also, they enabled Pingit to take advantage of QR promotional codes that small businesses kept near tills. Many more post-launch updates are planned. As Jenkins says 'We could have spent six months researching the idea or just put it out in the market and work it out from there. We didn't just innovate for the customer, we innovated how we do innovation.'

Looking at the story of Barclay's Pingit, we see many facets of innovation: a team working fast, confident in their gut, making ideas real during the development phase and even after launch. The spirit of 'making it real' was underpinned by the tone Jenkins set for the development programme. 'I had to be open to doing things differently. I'm not smart enough to do this on my own, I don't have the answers, we had to do this together.' This spirit of humility is essential for fast-moving teams where listening and consideration are at a premium.

The project was led by Chief Operating Officer Shaygan Kheradpir, an experienced technologist previously Chief Information Officer and Chief Technology Officer of Verizon. Jenkins admits that, to innovate, you need outsiders with different experience.

Making things real can't be done slowly. Jenkins lit a fire under the team. Not just by pushing the deadline (he openly admits to being 'restlessly dissatisfied'), but by giving them a sense of purpose. 'We need something bigger than money as a purpose and it's easy to get complacent. There is no reason a 320-year-old bank should become a 330-year-old bank – look at Sony, Blockbuster and Nokia. Our purpose has to be to make lives better for our customers, solve this and everything else will look after itself.'

"

This spirit of humility is essential for fast-moving teams where listening and consideration are at a premium

What It Really Takes to Get Real

Making ideas real is driven by a state of mind, a belief that doing things quickly, imperfectly and with brutal honesty is the right thing to do.

So how can you get this 'state of mind'? Can you simply adopt a new attitude? It's not useful to instruct innovation newbies to suddenly believe in Realness if they have no experience of it. The brain doesn't work like that.

Better look to the old adage: 'Feelings follow behaviour'. If you can get people to behave or act 'real' and they can see its benefits – then after time they will believe 'real'. They'll become raving advocates – believers like me!

Making things real demands that we have a 'good enough' mindset, we seek the maximum number of iterations through having a tight budget, we work under the radar and we pay attention to our idea building behaviours.

1 Good enough

Good enough prototypes, models or simulations encourage comment and play. Something that's 'too finished' doesn't invite comment. Somehow if it's perfect, it's saying 'I don't need your help – I'm fine!' I have had to say to our make it real guys: 'That's too good, it looks too real – can you mess it up a bit please?'

See the incomplete circle – this is why great advertising or a good joke works. You get enough of the story to be able to finish it off quickly in your mind. Effectively you complete the circle in a microsecond and smile as you get the punchline. The thing is, you've done it yourself. That's a story you kind of think is your own now because there's a bit of you in it.

It's the same with an unfinished mock-up or simulation. It invites the viewer to step in and complete, or at least try to complete. Again you feel kind of attached to it now – you've been part of something. This is why prototypes shouldn't be perfect.

A funny thing happens when two people stop discussing things and make them real instead. Let's say two people pick up a prototype for the first time. One person may be disappointed. They had pictured it as more sleek and sexy than the thing they have in their hands. The next person feels differently – the prototype looks great to them, just as they had imagined. The point is that we describe new ideas through the spoken or written word. But each of us interprets words differently. We see things in our mind's eye differently. To innovators this can be very dangerous. How many times have you seen something for the first time only to exclaim: 'Well I didn't picture it like that!' Making simulations or mock-ups – as fast as possible, without worrying about perfecting them – this is a good way to overcome this 'mind's eye' problem. Soon everyone's seeing the same thing.

Many executives get very stressed at the thought of a 'good enough' approach to innovation. Maybe the idea of playing around with a model or simulation rather than a spreadsheet feels like it's going to be a waste of time? Somehow it doesn't feel very 'business-like' to experiment; maybe a bit too playful? It doesn't fit the self-image of efficient, elevator-pitch man.

Again, this is why we need to dive in fast with Realness. Asking your colleagues to take a break from the spreadsheets and just 'make it real' takes some guts. Asking smart people to loosen up and 'see where this takes us' – not easy. But believe me, very soon even the most sceptical sceptic will see how valuable the process is. But they have to experience it to believe it, not talk about it.

2 Lowest cost

Experimenting is based on formulating a hypothesis or a hunch, testing it, adapting the hunch based on the results of the test and then testing it all over again. The objective of experimenting is to design the maximum number of 'learn and adapt loops' before locking in an investment. So the formula is pretty simple:

more learning loops = more learning = better innovation

Innovation is really very practical. If you can get down the cost of making things real you'll be able to experiment more often and this virtually guarantees better innovation. So the formula can be simplified:

cut cost of experimenting = better innovation

If the cost of experimenting looks expensive then we're unlikely to throw ourselves into an iterative series of tests. Worse still, we set out to innovate and end up with just one giant loop of experimentation – all our eggs in one basket.

At ?What If! we're making things real everyday so we've needed to recruit and build a network of people with diverse skills. They can quickly write a script, find actors and make a mini movie simulating a new service. They are able to make a model, simulate an app, a new type of smoothie, a 'nearly real' credit card – whatever. They can do it overnight and they're not so precious that they don't mind ripping it up and starting again. We've found it important to have these folks in-house and on hand – this means 'making it real' has a low marginal cost to us, we can make things real anytime. If you don't have the appetite to build an in-house 'make it real' capacity, then appoint someone to build a network. There are many people in every city of the world who can help make things real.

66

You need to set up and organise so that you can do as many experiments per unit of time as possible ... small, lightweight teams that ... can do a lot of experiments per week or per month ... then you'll get a lot more invention from that.

Jeff Bezos, Amazon.com Founder and CEO, in an interview
with *Businessweek* (2004)

3 Stealth

Stealth is an important aspect of making things real because so many new ideas are born into opposition. Almost by definition, a successful business is a hostile environment for a new idea that has the impertinence to say 'Hey guys – you've got this all wrong'.

A 'Captain One Minute, Pirate the Next' has a mischievous glint in their eye. They know that to get innovation moving they have to just get moving. The more people they have to include in the decision to start – the less likely they'll be able to. I have worked with some companies crippled by the sheer volume of 'covering off' they have to do.

So 'Just Start' is the innovator's motto. This means you'll have to sneak around the system – go under the radar. Most successful organisations have found ways to tolerate this pirate behaviour.

Making it real at Google

At the Googleplex, Google's HQ in Mountain View, California, you can't help but notice the number of casual presentation spaces. Early stage innovation isn't managed at Google in a traditional reporting sense. Innovation unfolds in a more organic way. An engineer with an idea will need help making his or her idea real; this will often mean they need smart people to pull a few late night shifts coding the idea into a basic working prototype. They might grab a microphone, try to attract a crowd and share the starting idea they have. Google understand how food and drink facilitate conversation, so at 'Beer and Demos' engineers will drum up support for a project. However they achieve it, the idea is to create 'flocking'. Engineers who like the sound of the idea will lend a hand and all Google engineers have 20% 'free time' – this is a non-policed concept that opens up part of an engineer's week to experiment. Like this, ideas gather momentum in an underground and unmanaged way. Eventually the idea will wither or be built and taken to a project board. It's a philosophy that seems to work – Google launch about five new products a week! And far better to get on and nurture an idea to the point at which we can see if it's a weed or a flower than to endlessly discuss the ambiguous green shoot.

Starbucks realness

Howard Schultz, Starbucks CEO, tells an interesting story about the development of the Frappuccino, their successful iced coffee. The product was initially developed by a Starbucks District Manager in Southern California in response to a competitor who had a best-selling ice coffee. Eventually Starbucks threw its weight behind the idea and created what *Businessweek* named one of the products of the year in 1996. What is so interesting about the story is that the store manager knew that Starbucks was not supportive of the idea – to them it sounded 'more like a fast-food shake than something a true coffee lover would enjoy'. So she got hold of a blender and started creating her own iced coffees. Even when she presented it to Schultz he had reservations but agreed to get behind the project. As Schultz says:

66

*'Perhaps the most remarkable thing about this story
is that we didn't do any heavy-duty financial analysis
on Frappuccino beforehand. We didn't hire a blue-chip
establishment consultant who could provide 10,000 pages
of support material. We didn't even conduct what major
companies would consider a thorough test. No corporate
bureaucracy stood in the way of Frappuccino. It was a
totally entrepreneurial project, and it flourished within a
Starbucks that was no longer a small company.'*

Howard Schultz and Dori Jones Yang. *Pour Your Heart Into It.*
How Starbucks built a company one cup at a time. Hyperion (1999)

4 Best behaviour!

So a mindset of 'good enough', lowest cost and stealth – this is what an innovator needs to make things real. But all of this will be wasted if we can't use the sketch, model or mock-up to grow ideas. We need to have an expansive dialogue; throwing in ideas and suggestions to make the next iteration even better.

Unsurprisingly this is where things can come unstuck. Opening up to constant feedback, collaborating over and over – it's exciting and it's exhausting. Hearing commentary from other people on your latest prototype is hard, especially when it's critical. Sometimes you can lose the plot and snap back at your critic. At times like this the entire experimental process can be jeopardised. We need to be on our best behaviour.

> 66
>
> *A new idea is delicate. It can be killed by a sneer or a yawn; it can be stabbed to death by a joke, or worried to death by a frown on the right person's brow*
>
> Charles Brower

Imagine the scene: a pharmaceutical innovation team is looking at how to improve compliance (following doctors orders), let's say on an asthma drug. They're about to meet up with a bunch of teenage asthmatics and show them the new design inhaler that was mocked-up last night. It looks pretty crude but later in the day they'll be iterating another inhaler so they're going to have to pay attention to the teens reactions.

All of the team are excited – except one. One person, let's call him Arnold, is fuming. You see, last night the conversation was very heated, everyone wanted a particular design except Arnold. So today he feels embarrassed about the previous night. He's not convinced his colleagues rate him and has started to disengage from them.

This is not a good way for a team to be. Just one Arnold can upset the apple cart. It's pretty likely that this group will waste their time managing Arnold, or worse still appeasing him. In my experience an innovation team has limited energy. They need to invest some of this on their ability to function as a team with regular meetings and heart-to-heart conversations. But most of the team's 'energy reserve' needs to be focused on cracking the challenge. If just a single team member is disruptive, then more energy gets diverted to cracking the team dynamics. If this continues the team becomes a 'black hole' – effectively it implodes. This is quite a common dynamic and many people have unfortunately got used to working in Black Hole teams.

Innovation can be a high pressure sport and it's not unusual for innovation teams to be severely destabilised by a minority of badly behaved individuals. One answer could be to establish a clear behavioural contract within the team. These are simple agreements between team members detailing how they're going to behave together. The behavioural agreements the asthma innovation team above could have made are:

* **No Fester:** 'If I'm ever feeling bent out of shape I will say it immediately, I know that you guys will help me work through it.'

* **Customer's Eyes:** 'Every first comment I make about a new prototype will be through the eyes of a customer.'

* **Seek Value:** 'I'll seek the value in my colleagues' comments before I give my view.'

Think of the difference this could have made if our asthma team had signed up to one of these simple behavioural contracts. Even if Arnold had forgotten his agreements, the rest of the group would have had complete licence to address the breach with him. Moreover they can address it as a 'broken agreement' not a personality issue. A behavioural contract makes hard stuff easier to talk about.

Greenhousing

A useful innovator's tool is to 'greenhouse' ideas. This means to force the growth of an idea by looking for what's great about it, the DNA if you like, and building on that.

Fariq: *'Hey, we could save a lot of money if we cancelled the summer party this year.'*

Jenny: *'I like the idea of saving money, my build on your idea would be to hold a picnic instead and ask each team to prepare a dish, that might even be more fun than paying for caterers.'*

Maybe you were tempted to raise your eyebrows at Fariq's suggestion? Or maybe tell him it was a daft idea? You can't do that in the greenhouse. The rule is to lean in and build an idea. What's the DNA of the idea? How can we build on that? Starting the sentence with 'my build' ensures this. It's a useful trick. Hopefully Fariq feels great, he had a bit of the idea, he got listened to. And Jenny feels great – she still got to go to a party – and saved money.

I mentioned the behavioural contract at ?What If! Our promises are made with the objective of making us a great innovation partner to our clients. Feel free to steal them, they work very well:

Impact: We obsess with the end goal, never slaves to process.

Audacity: We hate mediocrity, we think big.

Passion: We have explosive drive and contagious energy.

Love: We are in it for the long term and will always do the right thing, even when things get tough.

Adventure: We deliberately step off the path and get to see what others don't.

Employment at our place is contingent on these behaviours. That means you get hired by them and you use them to guide decisions. They're very powerful innovation tools.

Let's Get Practical

The only way to start making things real is to have a go. If you like what you read in this chapter then gather your team and ask them the question: 'What can we make real now?'

Don't be concerned if you have no idea how to make it real. You don't need to know how to make something real, that's something a group of you can figure out. So don't self-censor, don't stop yourself suggesting that the team makes something real if it's not apparent how you are going to achieve it. There is no shame in the following:

'Hey, let's make it real, now.'

'Yeah, but how?'

'I don't know – but can you help me work that out?'

Remember that making things real takes guts and a faith that it's better to DO ALMOST ANYTHING than ENDLESSLY TALK about doing something.

Collision Course

Creating Space for Serendipity

In **30** seconds

If you only had 30 seconds I'd tell you:

The physical space around us has a big impact on the way we think and interact with each other.

◆

The configuration of our space at work can promote the collision of insights and ideas and it can accelerate a team's ability to work quickly. Innovators need to take an active interest in their space.

◆

The need to pee and the need to eat; these are two surprisingly powerful tools to force collision.

◆

Promoting microbursts of social interaction should be a managed activity. Spontaneity takes a lot of planning.

◆

Spaces for serendipity are full of clutter. Innovation is allergic to clean and tidy environments.

◆

Space should be both serious and playful but never solemn.

◆

Innovation needs flexible spaces; this means our environment has to be low cost.

◆

The best innovation environments are not created through traditional management channels but are self-organised.

Method is taking on packaged goods giants like P&G at their own game. Started in 2001 by Eric Ryan and Adam Lowry, the company has global sales of over $100m. Method's ecofriendly soaps and cleaning products, including washing up liquid and laundry detergent, have busted out of the staid design language of the category. Their sleek, colourful bottles are kept on display at home, not hidden under the sink. Some Method fans even give their products as gifts.

Walking around Method's San Francisco headquarters, what strikes me as genius is how they use their space to innovate. First off, I see walls of copious shelving, all bursting with weird and wonderful packaging designs collected from all over the world. As Lowry says: 'We're surrounded by things that make us think differently'. The walls are pure stimulus.

Next, I look at several 3D printers that Method's marketing guys have taught themselves to use. It seems Method has taken Peter Drucker's maxim – that business is really only about two things, marketing and innovation – to heart. The company outsources all other functions, leaving the marketing office central to the operation. But a marketing office with 3D printers? This means they can print a newly shaped bottle overnight, ready to show it to consumers the next morning. Figuring that 70% of launches fail in their sector, Method bypasses quantitative testing. Instead the company 'auditions' its 3D designs with consumers.

Method's space is designed for speed-to-market, and this is core to Ryan and Lowry's philosophy: 'We're good at rapid innovation in a market dominated by players who are big and slow', says Lowry. 'We can do twenty to thirty product iterations when our competitors can only do one round of research. And while we can get a product from idea to launch in 12 weeks, our competitors need a year, minimum.' The ability to move at speed makes things feel less of a risk; it means: 'we're willing to experiment with ideas the bigger players wouldn't'.

Finally, the people of Method put everything up on their walls. I really mean everything. From the stuff you'd expect, like their mission, all the way to marketing plans, results, issues – everything. They call this 'Thinking Out Loud'. It means there is very little hidden, locked away on hard drives or in the cloud. The walls are inviting. I'm not allowed to look too closely, of course, but it's clear from the way the desks are arranged that meetings at Method happen standing up, right in front of the walls. And we all know that a stand-up meeting is a fast meeting.

Adam is quick to point out that while 'we force everything into the open, even if it's confrontational, nothing is hidden away. It's our values that guide our response.' The last part of this sentence is critical. Organisations that wear their hearts on their sleeves need to be able to deal with the passion that this arouses.

Method has a strong values culture that helps its people to work fast. Two of their values stand out for me: First, 'What would MacGyver do?' *MacGyver* was a US TV series featuring a secret agent famous for solving complex issues with everyday items rather than a gun. So the message here is that being resourceful is important. And second, 'Keep Method Weird'. This is an instruction to avoid becoming like the 'big boys': stay human, keep moving fast and continue being different.

With their shelves of stimulus, the ability to experiment and walls of 'Thinking Out Loud', Method does a great job of using its space to promote serendipitous encounters. It would be hard to work there and not innovate.

Intuitively we know that when we get to work, all that we physically interact with (what we see, touch or smell) is in some way profoundly important. Space affects all of us deeply whether we realise it or not. Our moods, our behaviour and our ability to connect with others are all directly influenced by the spaces we work in.

But not all organisations are as cultured as Method about their space. Many large offices have a buzzing 'designer' reception area, but go onto the working floors and you'll find near silent open-plan spaces. Out-of-town, campus-style offices have recreated shops and cafés on the entrance floor but now employees are trapped in a bubble of sameness. And the trend for encouraging work at home further snuffs out the potential for serendipity. Sleeping, eating, living and working in the same space isn't a recipe for stimulation.

Looking deeper into the Method story, and having spent weeks and months in many different offices, we can extract a few practical guidelines for a 'serendipitous space'.

First, at work we can't rely on insight and ideas colliding naturally; we have to create structures that force these things to bump into each other. Second, the outside world needs to be deliberately imported into the office; serendipity needs the clutter of provocative stimulus. And third, if you've worked hard to recruit a diverse workforce, don't blow it by forcing them to work in exactly the same way. You need to keep fighting for a flexible space that allows people to either collaborate or get their heads down. In this chapter I'm going to explore these three themes of forcing collision, creating clutter and fighting for flexibility.

"

There is no doubt whatever about the influence of architecture and structure upon human character and action. We make our buildings and afterwards they make us.

Winston Churchill addressing the English Architecture Association in 1924

Forcing Collision

In 2000, Pixar acquired an old Del Monte canning plant in Emeryville, California, for its new home. Steve Jobs, an early stage investor in Pixar, threw out initial plans to create three separate units on the site each housing a different function. Instead he pulled everyone together with a design for one large building with a giant atrium at its heart. He decided to use 'space' to force people to collide. He figured that as there were some activities everyone had to do every day, he may as well use this as a tool to collide people and ideas.

66

Steve put the mailboxes, meeting rooms, cafeteria, and, most insidiously and brilliantly, the bathrooms in the centre – which initially drove us crazy – so that you run into everybody during the course of a day. [Jobs] realised that when people run into each other, when they make eye contact, things happen.

Brad Bird, Director of *The Incredibles* (sourced from Rao et al., 2008)

But when we tried Pixar's brave move for our ?What If! London offices, it was harder to replicate. Our toilets were in existing fixed locations and the landlord wasn't keen on this central loo idea. In the end, we bulldozed the galley kitchens on each floor of our building and created a central supersized farmhouse style kitchen on the ground floor for everyone to come to instead.

OK, so there's quite a walk to find a snack, but when you get to the kitchen you can flop down at the big table and start up a conversation with a colleague you might not have seen in a while. These random encounters always throw up useful information. It's here that we find out who is working on what project and what latest tool or technique they are trying out. It's the random nature of these meetings that makes them all the more useful. Bumping into people you'd never thought of talking to yields more unexpected information than just reaching out to your usual group of buddies at work. And sitting down, face to face with a mug of coffee in hand, the conversation flows in a far more stimulating and rewarding way than email can ever hope to achieve.

Collision can be physical, literally bumping into each other, but it can also be emotional. Eating together is a very powerful way to force this emotional collision. Take a look at the following two meals served up at work. Which do you think has the power to change the conversation, allow people to drop their guard and say what they really mean?

Or this one?

This one?

Our catering team at ?What If! is called 'Food Is Love'. Over a bowl of homecooked food, scooped from a large pot with a big ladle, it's incredible how much a team of even the most time-pressed executives will relax and tell each other what they really think. There is something about taking a break and sitting down to a homecooked meal that ignites a deeper conversation than a loveless sandwich can ever do.

Another way to force collision is to keep the food and drink at work as low-tech as possible. Picture this scene. Claudia, who runs our Food Is Love team announces she's going to bake a cake. The whole team stops what they are doing for a moment, lost in a micro burst of happiness as they anticipate this homemade delicacy. When she arrives with the cake, everyone drops what they're doing – they get up and hang out for a few minutes. In that time their current work is forgotten and they have an opportunity to catch up and have fun.

It is in these sideline conversations that so many good ideas brew. These are great opportunities to kick around ideas and observations that might be off the agenda or non-core. If you're not going to unburden yourself over a homebaked cake and cup of tea, then when are you? Contrast this scene with depressing food and drink dispensing units that so many offices have installed. In my view, it's better to invest in constant micro social gatherings rather than cut costs installing soulless mechanical devices.

If you're not going to unburden yourself over a homebaked cake and cup of tea, then when are you?

Encouraging people to hot desk, or to sit wherever they want in an office, forces people to collide. This is especially useful for innovation. If you have the technology that supports working in different locations and can keep project collateral in some central location, then sitting in a different place at work each day is a great recipe for serendipity. In my experience it's not possible to have a 100% hot desk environment at work. It does make a lot of sense for some people to sit next to each other. But even potentially mobile people resist hot desking. I think this comes from a natural desire to 'nest'. This should be challenged as many people don't need files, in-trays or 'stuff' anymore and the benefits of serendipitous encounters will always outweigh the comfort of nesting.

This is one of the floors at ?What If! Every day, people find a new space and have new colleagues to get to know. These tables are in effect pockets of collision.

Valve is a 300-person strong software company behind game hits such as *Half-Life*, *Counter Strike* and *Portal*. They take the idea of hot desks literally. Their desks have wheels enabling them to move their entire workstation to be co-located with their project team. As their company handbook says 'Think of those wheels as a symbolic reminder that you should always be considering where you could move yourself to be more valuable.'

Forcing people to collide means we need people to 'mingle'. This is a great word. It means to 'bring or mix together or with something else usually without fundamental loss of identity' (Merriam-Webster's dictionary). This is exactly what lies at the heart of serendipity. The more people are social, the more they bring their individual characteristics to the party, and so the more they build a set of trusting relationships. The more they trust, the more they open up. This is the primordial soup of innovation.

So if you can't rip out all the toilets at work or create a giant farmhouse kitchen, there are other non-physical ways to encourage mingling. They are extremely powerful at getting humans to connect – and at a profound level. The good news is that they are all lots of fun and virtually free.

Innocent, the famous UK-based smoothie maker and now part of The Coca-Cola Company, believe in mingling, which is shown by their many social clubs. There's the Cake Club, the Gardening Club, the Cycling Club, the Cake Decorating Club (a splinter group from the Cake Club), the Cheese Club and many more clubs. But why invest in helping employees spend time together in such clearly non-work related activities?

> The answer hit me when one of the team at Innocent explained that when you get together over something you're passionate about, like cake decorating, you forget you're with a colleague. As you swap stories and enjoy each other's company, you become lost in the thing you like doing. The Cake Club builds trusting relationships across different departments. So when you're innovating and desperate for a favour, you know who to call. It's kind of hard to say no to someone when you've spent the previous evening together perfecting your piping technique.

Opening up, revealing a bit more about yourself – this is how relationships are formed. There's a terrific way to accelerate this process between colleagues at work called PechaKucha.

The idea behind PechaKucha (which means the sound of 'chit chat' in Japanese) was developed in Tokyo in 2003 by Astrid Klein and Mark Dytham (Klein Dytham Architecture) as an event to showcase the work of young designers. PechaKucha is an effective and novel way to accelerate the ability of work colleagues to build trusting relationships. It has followers all over the world and at ?What If! we run a PechaKucha session on one evening each month. The rules are simple: get a group of colleagues together after work. Beer in hand, they listen to a colleague give a presentation. But this is a presentation with a difference. It can be about anything that the speaker can talk about with passion, there are twenty slides and each takes no more than 20 seconds. So a 20 × 20 seconds presentation takes just under 7 minutes. There is no time to get nervous or even prepare. This means many more people have a go at speaking than would normally do so. During the session we might hear from four or five colleagues and the whole thing takes no more than an hour.

Last time I went to our ?What If! PechaKucha session I heard about Rosie's trip across Russia in a beaten-up old VW. I heard about the flower shop that Matthew opened. I heard about Sam's obsession with base-jumping (jumping off high buildings with a parachute). These were great stories, revealing and intimate and all in 20 × 20 seconds. I never knew those things about those guys and in a short space of time I got an incredible insight into what made them tick. Maybe over time I would have got to know this about them but it accelerated our relationship and meant that in the following months we were able to be more frank with each other and work faster together.

Creating Clutter

Method, as we've heard about, talks about 'Thinking Out Loud'. They populate the walls of their offices with interesting packaging, progress updates on projects and latest performance indicators. A space that's a kaleidoscope of thinking, concepts and customer comments is very stimulating. This type of space isn't neat and tidy. Here, clutter is good.

Remember the new kitchen we built at ?What If!? We also ensured that the walk to the kitchen went right through one of our Make It Real teams. They built shelves to display their latest prototypes. Now it's not possible to spend more than an hour in the office without picking up the latest new-new thing.

A space that shouts 'Hey, pick up this latest prototype' or 'Look at this new concept – what do you think?' is not a solemn or sober place. An office like this needs to communicate that 'in here, we don't take ourselves too seriously'. Clinically clean offices with no inkling of who the consumer is or what innovation is in the pipeline, do not generate serendipity.

Deliberately placing 'fun stuff' in an office sets the tone. It gives people permission to engage with each other in a playful and humorous way.

This is 'The Wheel of Decision Making' in Innocent's offices. If you're not sure what decision to make then spin it and it will make the decision for you.

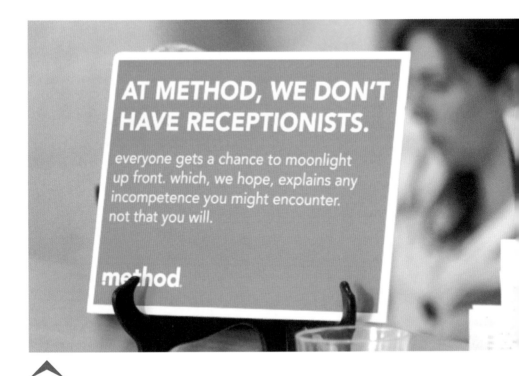

This is the reception desk at Method's HQ in San Francisco. To me it's confident, amusing and says a lot about them.

66

Offices need symbols of levity. Reminders that while we take work seriously, we don't take ourselves seriously

This is an exercise bike that doubles as a fruit blender in Google's London office.

We have a cow in our London and New York offices. There's no real purpose to it but, similarly to Innocent's decision wheel, Google's blender bike and Method's reception, the cow is a symbol of levity. It says that while we take work seriously, we don't take ourselves seriously.

So, just as space can stimulate conversation and lighten the mood, it can ground us in our customers and remind us every minute of every day who really pays our salaries.

UKTV, a major multichannel provider in the UK, has used its space as a reminder about the viewers of their popular TV channel Dave (as the tagline says: 'The Home of Witty Banter'). Meetings held in this room have a constant reminder about who is viewing and what their interests are.

Using space to communicate who your consumers are and what drives them isn't restricted to meeting rooms. Here, the boardroom of a major European retail chain was redecorated to reflect the lifestyle of its customers – in this case teenage girls. There was no doubt that decisions taken in this boardroom were influenced by the decoration.

The boardroom table

Making TV real

A leading broadcaster asked us to help create better TV programmes for children. Instead of presenting our ideas in PowerPoint, we took a boring meeting room in the broadcaster's head office and re-created it as a children's classroom. But we didn't stop there. We hired an actress to play a teacher and six 8-year-olds to play pupils. They played out a script we had developed, which was a 'classroom' discussion focused on the impact children's broadcasting had on the pupils.

We made the busy TV executives sit on the small chairs at the back of the 'class'. Initially they were sceptical: 'You're asking me to sit on a child's chair and watch a play!' But they soon saw the value in our performance, it was a great way to bring to life the programming issues they were struggling with. In fact, so rapt were they that they asked for the performance to be repeated and even questioned some of the pupils – forgetting they were actors. After the 'show' our recommendations were accepted. The use of the meeting space had a fundamental effect on the project.

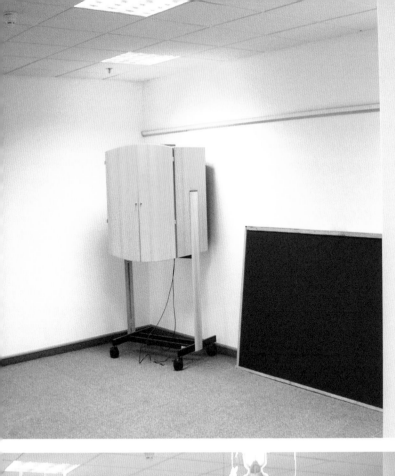

Fighting for Flexibility

I spend a lot of time with executives looking at their workspace and I've been lucky enough to have toured some of the world's most incredible offices – and some of the worst as well. To get a better idea of how people want to work, I will ask them to draw me a picture of their ideal working environment. Forget about the office I say, just draw whatever comes to mind.

This is a typical picture people draw to describe their ideal work environment. It's telling us that different places are needed at different times of the day for different tasks. There are internet café type places where comfortable but uninterrupted work is done. There are open spaces where people can get outside. There are intimate coffee shop type spaces where two people can get something off their chest. And there is plenty of movement between the spaces. So, to innovate, our space needs to be flexible.

Very often, innovators feel like they battle for even a small degree of flexibility. Most office spaces are designed and managed by professional facilities managers who are working to a different agenda. Innovators want flexible spaces, they want messy spaces and they want to bring outsiders into the office. They may want to work at odd hours and they can't predict how their workspace needs will change over the next few months. For a buildings manager, this is about as bad as it gets. They have a finite budget, many stakeholders other than the innovators and they have health and safety codes. The battle between the innovators who want to change the space and the building manager who wants to maintain the space is a common source of friction.

The good news is that flexible spaces shouldn't cost the earth. In fact, they cannot. The more you invest in expensive office equipment and floor plans, the less likely you are to change them. There are many stories of how cramped, uncomfortable and 'disposable' offices have contributed to great innovation. Some of the most innovative periods in Pfizer's history coincided with ramshackle buildings in Sandwich, Kent, in the UK. For a low cost but effective approach to the work enviornment go to Pixar where they have constructed a series of garden sheds inside their Emeryville HQ. These are a low cost and fun way to create flexible meeting and focused working spaces.

Innovators Crave Flexible Spaces

Sometimes they need to concentrate.

Sometimes they need a place to stick all their thinking on the walls and lock out the rest of the world.

Sometimes they need a comfortable space where colleagues can get together and play with new ideas.

Sometimes they need an intimate and private space to confide in each other.

Fight for Flexibility: Space to Concentrate

The original cubicle designer, Robert Prost, recently issued an apology lamenting his unwitting contribution to what he called 'monolithic insanity'. But don't torch those Dilbert cubicles just yet; they're great to concentrate in.

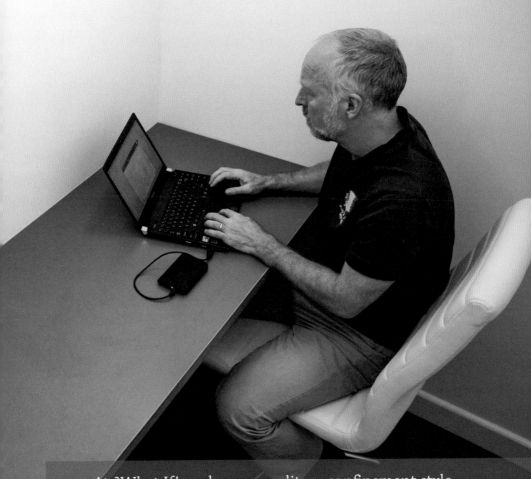

At ?What If! we love our solitary confinement style
spaces – ideal for getting stuff done

Fight for Flexibility: An Incident Room

A permanent base where you can stick up clues and get the team together to connect them. Commandeer a meeting room and make it your own. This is the place all the collateral of a project should be kept. It's also a place you can invite guests to help build the case.

These rooms need to be secure from prying eyes and overzealous office cleaners.

Fight for Flexibility: A Creative Space

Innovation teams need to spend lots of time together. A large room with access to natural light and the ability to make things real is ideal. This room can be set up on a temporary basis.

Creative spaces don't work if they are dark or uncomfortable. A bright and comfortable environment makes you want to kick your shoes off, smile, sit back and dream a little. You need to work hard at getting the environment right to make this happen.

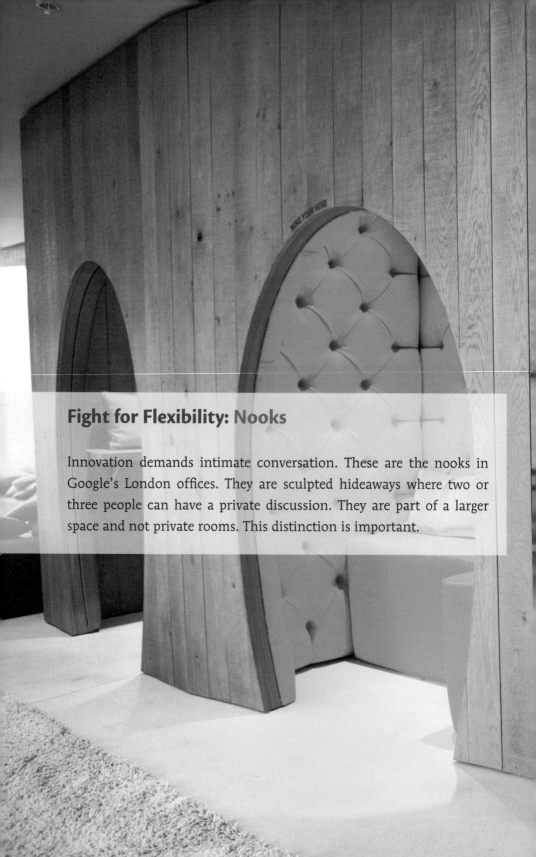

Fight for Flexibility: Nooks

Innovation demands intimate conversation. These are the nooks in Google's London offices. They are sculpted hideaways where two or three people can have a private discussion. They are part of a larger space and not private rooms. This distinction is important.

For nook, think cave. The idea is that you feel totally protected from behind and above whilst having a good view of the 'outside world'.

A good way to get the most flexible space for serendipity is to reframe it as a do-it-yourself activity and not a management initiative. Colleagues who design their space generally create a mix of social and 'head down' spaces. They spend less money than professional office outfitters and they feel more engaged as a result.

Pimp my cubicle

Zappos (derived from 'Zapatos' meaning 'shoes' in Spanish) is the world's largest online shoe retailer. Founded in 1999, the $2bn revenue Nevada-based company was recently acquired by Amazon.

Under the leadership of CEO Tony Hsieh, Zappos has become a model for service organisations the world over. So great is the demand to visit and understand 'how they do it' that Zappos runs an executive learning programme based on its practices. Zappos has really stretched the service model I have seen work effectively at South West Airlines, John Lewis Partnership, HSBC's First Direct and IKEA:

1. Be clear about the main thing (for Zappos it's great service. There is no limit for time on a call with a customer – the record so far is eight hours).

2. Have leaders with a knack for communication (the exec team sit on 'Monkey Row' open plan desks right in the middle of the Head Office).

3. Get the right people in (during the initial training at the company you are offered $4000 to walk away, 97% refuse).

4. Encourage a fun and engaging culture ('Zapponians' are exhorted to believe in 'fun and a little weirdness').

5. Happy employees will make happy customers and happy customers will tell other customers.

This is the success formula for any service organisation; Zappos do it particularly well and the physical environment has played a big part in their success. At the heart of the job is the ability to interact with a customer in a positive and helpful manner. This means they need to act the same way with their colleagues and their workspace needs to feel friendly, fun and full of zest for life. Zapponians are given the budget to decorate their own spaces and meeting rooms. The company values of 'play' and 'a little weirdness' give licence to really get creative.

Ultimately, a physical space that reflects the business model keeps everyone on the same page; it means everyone wants to tell the Zappos story. To have all staff engaged behind the big picture and taking responsibility for the little details is a prize that most corporations would dearly love to win.

CEO Tony Hsieh, at his desk.

The University of Exeter in the UK explored the link between whether employees get to have a say in the design of their workspace and productivity. In an experiment, people were asked to undertake tasks across differing working environments. Those able to design and decorate their own environment scored a whopping 32% increase in productivity vs. people told to work in a bland room.

Dr Craig Knight, who led the study (University of Exeter, 2010) comments: 'When people feel uncomfortable in their surroundings they are less engaged, not only with the space but also with what they do in it. If they can have some control, people report being happier at work, identifying more with their employer, and are more efficient when doing their jobs.'

66

Those able to design and decorate their own environment scored a whopping 32% increase in productivity vs. people told to work in a bland room

Let's Get Practical

Creating space for serendipity can't be an isolated task. Think back to Method. The joint CEOs were huge advocates of their space and their values amplified how their space worked. For Method, space strategy is right at the heart of the organisation. So to prevent space improvements becoming tokenistic or just a single lick of paint, build into the next annual plan a section on space strategy and how it supports the growth agenda.

If you're going to upgrade your space along the lines I've suggested, one of the first stops is your buildings or facilities manager. These people have tough jobs. On the one hand they are trying to make a building safe and contain costs and on the other they have to contend with annoying people like me who say things like 'let's make this messier, let's leave all our insights on the walls for a month, let's get our prototypes out into the open'. Getting their support is an important task.

Finally, it might be easier to take a section of the office or a department and in the spirit of 'making it real' just get on and make some changes. Ask your colleagues to take an active role. And don't forget the cakes!

5

Battling the Corporate Machine

Navigating Naysayers and the Inevitable
Organisational Roadblocks

30

In

seconds

If you only had 30 seconds I'd tell you:

Pushing an idea through an organisation is much harder than having the idea in the first place. Sometimes it can feel like the battle is within your business rather than out in the marketplace.

◆

How an innovation challenge is framed sets it up for success later on. We need to know how much innovation is needed, what type of innovation and by when.

◆

Similarly the innovation challenge needs to be scoped at the outset. The more we can define what is in and out of scope, the less others will make limiting assumptions.

◆

Leaders who demonstrate a love for their products cut through bureaucracy.

◆

It's not possible to innovate if your mind is elsewhere. Create essential 'headspace' though a focused and exciting rallying cry.

◆

A big company needs innovation safe zones.

◆

At work the grapevine is underestimated as a force for accelerating or destroying innovation. Your reputation as a good listener can magnetise good ideas and people to you.

◆

Normal accounting metrics don't work for innovation. Instead innovation measures need to inspire a rich dialogue between innovators and their sponsors.

◆

Finally, organisations will always have naysayers; instead of getting depressed about these glass-half-empty people, innovators relish the challenge of winning them over.

'If you want to install videoconferencing, I can get back to you in a couple of months, after we've talked to our approved suppliers. And if you want to put anything on the walls, you need to go to the Building Standards Committee.' Pierre, the new Chief Innovation Officer at a global retailer, couldn't believe what he was hearing. All he wanted to do was set up an innovation incident room for one of his projects. To add to this, during the previous week, several heads of department had called him to warn him off using their people on innovation projects. Pierre could deal with a passive-aggressive environment, but this felt more like open warfare.

'Can you just ...' Karen didn't even hear the end of the sentence. She'd had enough of 'can you justs'. It seemed to her that she could spend all day running around writing presentation after presentation for senior executives wanting to know more about her innovation project. To Karen it felt like the whole business was caught up chasing its tail. Someone somewhere needed to call 'STOP' and re-focus on moving innovation ahead rather than on show-and-tell.

Yoon was incredibly excited when he took the innovation job; he felt like a lucky guy as he whistled to work on his first day. His first meeting with his project managers notched his excitement levels up even more; he was going to get them out of the office where they could think freely. 'We have a blank canvas', he told them, 'it's up to us to now, we'll meet in a month's time. Who knows where we'll get to but I'm really looking forward to working with you guys.' Yoon's rousing speech got more than polite applause. His next meeting was with his finance director, and Yoon's heart almost stopped at the FD's opening salvo: 'Before you go on your little jaunt I need to see five-year projections for these projects. I need to know the impact on the bottom line'.

> **Sometimes it feels like the innovation battle isn't being fought in the marketplace: it's being fought at home – against the corporate machine**

Pierre, Karen and Yoon; the names are changed but the stories are true. Sometimes it feels like the innovation battle isn't being fought in the marketplace: it's being fought at home – against the corporate machine. Even when a company's leadership sets innovation as a priority, the corporate machine sometimes seems to work against rather than for this goal. This may not be apparent at the outset, but the naysayers, those who only see the worst of a situation, reveal their true colours as time goes by. And some organisations are downright antagonistic; innovation is seen as a career threat. I've seen a lot of these fights. They look pretty similar whatever industry you're in. Sometimes it can feel like you're swimming through treacle. This phrase amuses my US colleagues where treacle translates to molasses. So picture swimming through molasses if that helps. Another graphic illustration for how innovation really feels is the board game 'Snakes and Ladders'. Many innovators describe their journey as starting from 0 in the bottom left, aiming for 100 in the top right, sometimes a ladder will accelerate you forwards but most often an unexpected snake will suck you backwards.

In the early part of this exciting innovation journey we see individuals and small teams working together in extraordinary ways. As an idea becomes more formed, many more people get involved. Suddenly everyone is interested in our great idea, but this just slows things down. Our 'Captain One Minute, Pirate the Next' needs all his or her cunning to hold things together and push ideas 'over the line'.

The key is to set things up at the start so that the corporate machine can move swiftly and capitalise on serendipity. Innovation needs to be carefully framed and scoped at the outset. Innovators need to manage their reputation so that they attract ideas and assistance from the corporate machine. They need to obsess about their products and not their process – they need to create headspace, safe zones and the right metrics. These are just some of the tactics needed to overcome the inevitable roadblocks. The watchwords are anticipation, stealth and tenacity. But most of all, the answer is not to try and fight bureaucracy with more meetings and more presentations. Instead you keep things simple, turn up the plain-speaking dialogue and fight for what's right for your customer.

Setting Innovation Up for Success

Innovation is a rolling fireball and within it a series of mini experiments are always firing off. Sometimes we learn from them in time to make a change, sometimes we learn from them but don't do enough soon enough. The fireball will either pick up speed and explode into a successful launch or gradually lose its heat, slow down and extinguish in an ignominious puff of smoke. Innovation really is a thriller!

Think of how we might frame a painting. The frame denotes the edges of the picture, we take care to hang the frame in the best possible light and in the best place so that the audience will get the most out of it. This is a useful way of looking at innovation, as the roots of innovation failure (the ignominious puff of smoke) can often be traced to the very early days – right back to the 'set-up' of the challenge. From the outset innovation needs to be carefully framed, the organisation needs to know how important it is and what is in and out of scope. Without this framing, people will make their own assumptions about innovation. Some will think it's important – others will dismiss it as a 'nice to have' activity. Some will assume that innovation is about twists and tweaks to products and services, whilst others will assume it's about disruptive and game-changing activity. Framing the challenge sets innovation up for success.

Recently I was running an innovation strategy workshop with the board of a multibillion dollar company. I asked the CEO how important innovation was. His answer was 'very', and he added that 'we've innovated every element of production and distribution, there's no more to come from there'. I pushed him to quantify how much growth was needed from innovation. He conferred with his CFO and reported that even if they made the acquisitions they were planning and even if they worked their socks off – there was still a £1bn revenue gap over the next 4 years. He didn't believe in back-loading the plan so he needed £250m revenue from innovation within the year. As the penny dropped, the rest of the board gave a collective gulp. This wasn't really new news, but it was the first time that it had been expressed to them in such stark terms.

So, in the story above when I asked the CEO to state how much innovation he needed he subtracted 'normal growth' revenue and planned acquisition revenue from the revenue target set by his shareholders. The gap felt like a chasm. The CEO was also able to frame the type of innovation he needed. He was looking for revenue, so innovating with new products, pricing and routes to market were more important to him than innovating more cost-efficient ways of working. He was also able to frame the timescale behind innovation. These are the bedrocks of framing an innovation challenge:

* How much?

* What type?

* By when?

So calling out the 'growth gap' is an essential first step in framing the innovation challenge. How much revenue or profit does innovation have to deliver? If the number is significant, then innovation gets established as a core element of high-level strategy. Being clear about the growth gap is effectively an insurance policy against innovation becoming an orphan within the organisation.

Another important way to set innovation up for success is to scope it clearly. I've experienced supposed 'disruptive' challenges expressed in such a level of detail that there was no real licence to look over the horizon and really re-think the business. As a result, what was supposed to be a breakthrough innovation is seen by the customers as nothing more than an unexciting twist. I've experienced challenges that aren't explicit about constraining factors until they've shown themselves much too late for us to do anything about them. If you've ever thought to yourself 'Why the hell didn't you tell me that at the beginning?' then you'll know what I mean. I've also experienced innovation defined at such a level of abstraction that the project became an unfocused 'boil the ocean' type project. These projects invariably implode with the overwhelming number of options faced.

To illustrate the value of clever scoping, I want to take you to an unlikely place. It is 1982, 'Eye of the Tiger' by Survivor is number one in the US and the UK music charts, and I've just bought my first car. Hardly a muscle car, the quirky two cylinder Citroen 2CV was designed in France in the 1930s and nine million were produced between 1948 and 1991. Originally the 2CV came with a pull cable to start and no door locks. My version had removable seats (for picnics) and foldup windows. It took me several minutes to accelerate to a top speed of 60 mph. Driving along, singing away, I was king of the road! Here I am in 1982, proud owner of The Beast in a classic 'my first car' photo. My little sister Zoë was clearly aware of the importance of the occasion.

The interesting thing about this car is how clearly the innovation was scoped. Pierre-Jules Boulanger, Citroen's design chief, told his designers they were about to create the simplest and cheapest car possible – he called it an 'umbrella on wheels'. Boulanger told his team that the new car must be able to take a farmer and his family along muddy tracks without breaking a basket of eggs placed on the back seat. Passengers had to be able to wear both clogs and hats in comfort. On the open road it had to reach 60 km/h (just under 40 miles/h) and cost no more than a third of its nearest competitor.

In 1948, when production started, the 2CV was panned by critics as ugly, but the people of France loved it. The waiting list was 2 years long and the design remained more or less unchanged for an unprecedented 40 years.

The scoping of the innovation brief for the 2CV was brilliant. It managed to hit a useful level of detail and yet it afforded the designers huge licence to experiment. The brief was clear about a couple things – the ride quality and the price, but otherwise open ended. Creativity loves these kinds of constraints. The focus of the development was now on breaking all the rules of suspension design and lightweight engine manufacture. The Citroen 2CV was a truly innovative vehicle.

A practical way to scope an innovation challenge is to force an exploration of expanded or contracted versions of the brief. Start by writing down the initial definition of the challenge in the middle of a page. In the photo on the next page, taken from our work with a train company, the original challenge was 'to improve first class seats'. The team was able to expand the challenge by asking a very simple question: 'Why?' Answering this enabled them to ladder up the challenge and broaden the scope. Now they had some potential bigger and broader definitions of the challenge. Then by answering 'How?' they were able to contract the challenge. Now they had tighter and more specific definitions. Each of these new definitions opens up exciting new perspectives on

WHY?
- Trade second class passengers up to First Class...

- Improve the profitability of first-Class...

- Offer a seamless premium travel experience from door-to-door...

IMPROVE FIRST CLASS SEATS!

HOW?
- How can we offer multifunctional seating (sleep, working....)?

- Can we build advertising into each seat?

- Can we offer 'sofa seating' like posh cinemas do?

the challenge and spawns a raft of new ideas. I'm always amazed at how even small alterations to the definition of an innovation challenge can have such a big impact on the scope of the project and the ideas it will deliver. Asking 'Why?' and 'How?' – innovation tools don't come simpler or more effective than this.

There's no rule that says an expanded or contracted definition is best. The key is that you force the exploration of alternative definitions and you do it early.

But even with a clear definition of our challenge, it's too easy for a group of people to make assumptions about what is in and out of scope. It's important to confront assumptions early on. You may not think you need to because you believe that everyone is on the 'same page', but this is in itself a dangerous assumption.

We were once working with a retail bank on the customer proposition and commercial model of the 'bank of the future'. Disruptive projects like these can quickly spin out of control unless the whole team gets clear on how much they need to stretch and agree what is in scope and out of scope.

At the outset of the project we gathered a group of particularly influential stakeholders in a large meeting room. We surprised them by asking them to stand around a rope lying on the floor and coiled into a circle. Prior to this session we had asked everyone to scribble down ideas for a bank of the future – they had to dream up and write down obvious ideas and plenty of radical ones too. The ?What If! team had done extra homework. We had scoured the planet for interesting new ideas and businesses. Everyone had brought along their homework and I decided to go first with my most radical idea, one that I was sure would be rejected as too 'way out'. I held up a piece of paper with the headlines of my idea; the bank closed all its products down and instead became a financial services 'finder'. Promising personalised service, the bank would be a kind of human comparison site as it took a brief from its customers, scoured the market for the right products and got them the best deal from which it took a finder's fee. I braced myself for howls of derision, but they didn't come. 'That's not as daft as it might sound' said one banker. Another had more support: 'I hadn't thought of that but I think we should look at it – we shouldn't be constrained by the type of business we are today.'

There followed quite a debate and eventually my idea was placed inside the circle, it was 'in scope'. The debate had informed the project team about how the stakeholders were thinking and what level of risk they were prepared to tolerate. Time flew by as we dissected and argued over the next 20 or so ideas. By the end of the session some ideas lay inside the rope and some outside. Now we had a very clear sense of what was in and out of scope. As they left, the stakeholders commented on how invigorating it was to be talking about 'real things' rather than debating hypotheses. The simple act of getting people to stand around a coiled rope and debate what goes inside and outside is always effective. The standing rather than sitting, the physical placing of an idea inside or outside – somehow this injects real energy and camaraderie into the process.

In order for a scoping session to work, it's essential that the key players show up and don't simply send their delegates instead. Entice bona fide stakeholders to this meeting by insisting the project cannot start without them. Flatter them, coerce them, stamp your foot, tempt them with food – whatever works for you – you need the real players present. And make sure they don't censor. They need to bring along the widest ranging collection of possible paths and ideas. The idea is to 'let it all hang out' – no matter how radical or impractical the thought.

We have found a surprising number of benefits to these simple scoping exercises. They:

- Encourage a wide group of stakeholders to 'dump' every idea they've ever had. This cathartic experience means they feel listened to and are less likely to sabotage the process later on with the continual reappearance of their favourite idea.

- Force the project team to expand their horizon. Maybe the answer lies in a new business model, working with a new partner, or distributor?

- Spotlight potential winning ideas – and early on.

- Help the project team to understand the calibre of their innovation colleagues and stakeholders.

- Expose divisions within the group; this type of intelligence is essential.

Love Thy Product

Kingfisher is the largest global DIY retail group outside the US. The £10bn group trades as B&Q in China and the UK, Screwfix in the UK, Castorama across France, Russia, Spain and Poland, a joint venture with Kockas in Turkey and a strategic partnership with Hornbach in Germany.

In 2008, Ian Cheshire was appointed CEO and moved innovation high up the agenda. Cheshire appointed B&Q Board Director

Andy Wiggins to a new role – Group Innovation Director. Wiggins comments that 'Ian's view was that at the outset of a venture like this, how could one define "good"? Ian's counsel was to accept the ambiguity of the situation and just start doing what I felt was right and made it clear he would back me to work in this way. I found this both liberating and initially unsettling but ultimately the right way to approach the problem, with the flexibility to try things out and go in the direction of the energy.'

Together Wiggins and Cheshire built an innovation path designed for speed. First, a team of creative facilitators would work with suppliers, entrepreneurs and customers to create new process or product idea platforms. Next a 'Dragons Den' of four board members would hear business pitches from idea champions around the business. They had a multimillion pound pot earmarked for innovation and the power to release funds fast. Then a Pilot and Delivery Team of about eight operational leaders would ensure ideas were fast tracked as pilots in a few stores. These could be new retail models, new service ideas or new products.

Four years after Cheshire pushed the innovation button, Kingfisher's stock has doubled in value to £7.2bn, shareholders have seen returns of 126% whilst the FTSE has seen a mere 16%. This is despite the severe slump in most European economies during the same time period. Some of Kingfisher's performance will have come from integration savings and greater buying power as it has expanded, but innovation has played a critical role.

Today in B&Q or a Castorama you can take DIY classes. Don't know how to lay tiles? Just scan the Quick Read code on the shelf and watch a video on your smartphone about estimating, laying and grouting tiles. You can hire self-drive vans in case you end up buying more than you'd planned. Getting married? Try the B&Q Wedding List – it's online. There are eco-shops and eco-audits helping you manage your energy consumption. You can buy click-together patio decking and fencing and even a space-saving toilet, which incorporates a hand basin and taps. Within four years Kingfisher has evolved from a struggling retailer to a fast-growing, global and innovation-led business.

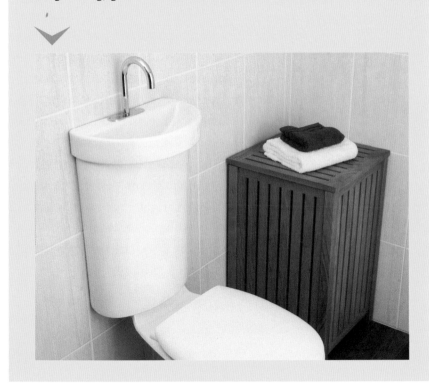

I think the Kingfisher group's story is highly instructive. To get things moving in a large organisation senior executives need to be highly engaged (and be seen to be highly engaged) with their products. Hearing the Kingfisher executives talk about their business, there's no doubt that they think product (and so customer) before process.

66

*Most people
will apply the
same process to
innovation as they
do to ordering
paper clips – a
bucketload of
procurement
and return on
investment
processes*

A leader who is deeply engaged with the output of his or her company, and is known for this, can really accelerate innovation. Whilst most broadcaster revenues are shrinking during the current economic crunch, UKTV's revenues have been growing year on year. CEO Darren Childs attributes this to their ability to move fast and to innovate. As he says, 'most people will apply the same process to innovation as they do to ordering paper clips – a bucketload of procurement and return on investment processes.' Childs attributes the key to speeding the flow of ideas at UKTV to his focus on the programme making and not the process: 'I take a massive interest in product, I can move things through management fast – I can green light things on the spot'. Childs adds that: 'A passion for your product can really make a difference for the CEO; I can really help build the future of the company by speeding good ideas up.'

Headspace

J. K. Rowling's *Harry Potter* stories introduced us to the 'Dementors'. They are soulless creatures considered to be the foulest beings on Earth. They are ghoulish fiends who suck your soul and, as their name suggests, cause people who encounter them for too long to lose their minds. If you've not seen the Dementors at work, then you should. They're also a great metaphor for how innovation can often feel in big business.

Many innovators in large organisations report the Dementor effect. They can't seem to find the time or the energy to get immersed in their innovation projects. In order to discover new things, there comes a point when innovators have to get out of the office and lose themselves in fresh stimulus. This deliberate dislocation is essential and if your mind is constantly distracted it won't happen. Over time, innovators lose their mojo and have less and less stamina to battle the corporate machine. Without realising it their innovation projects drift into mediocrity. This innovation doom-loop is not uncommon.

One of the most common reasons for this soul sucking is the sheer volume of reporting. A common complaint is that leaders are out of touch with how far their voice carries, how it distorts and how much headspace the smallest request can take up. Another reason is the company's addiction to a world of possibilities. It's easy to start too many projects. One of my clients reported feeling like 'the sky is black with planes – each is a project but there's no space for them to land and all the time more are taking off'. Some people complain of too many silos and of the depression at finding someone just a few metres away has been working on the same thing as them.

Whatever the reason for this lack of energy, innovators need the right 'headspace'. They need to have the right combination of positive attitude and clear focused time. A story that best demonstrates alignment, passion and clarity comes from Unilever. This story is close to my heart (although I can't take any credit for it) as I started my career working as a trainee marketer on Unilever's laundry brands.

Unilever has traditionally held strong detergent market share positions with brands like Persil, Omo, Breeze, Surf and Skip in just about every country of the world apart from the US where Procter & Gamble rules the detergent markets. Washing powder, or liquid, is a product like petrol. You don't want it for itself but for the things it can do for you. It's tough to create a sense of 'specialness' with products like these and, for many years, detergent brands had been stuck in an old-fashioned comparison of clean versus 'really clean' clothes.

In 2000, a small global brand group called 'Top Clean' was established within Unilever under the leadership of David Arkwright. Their remit was to breathe life into Unilever's portfolio of high-performance detergent powders and liquids globally.

Initially Arkwright gathered a small team in Unilever's London HQ. They promised each other that they would work in a new way. They would get out of the office and get under the skin of how consumers (mostly mums) really thought and talked about detergent. They would not be afraid to propose new marketing concepts, however disruptive they might appear. Arkwright's team sensed this was a market that was in need of something very different to the tired messages about biological or bleach cleaning.

Some months later the Top Clean team came across an advertising campaign Unilever was running in Canada for Sunlight, a brand of fabric detergent. The tag-line 'Go Ahead, Get Dirty' promoted a devil-may-care attitude to life, something that was a dramatic departure from the usual 'whiter than white' cleaning messages. Sales of Sunlight in Canada were going through the roof.

Inspired, the Top Clean team set about trying out new brand messages that explored a more libertarian attitude to parenting. The new message to mums was radical: 'Let your kids enjoy their childhood. Let them get dirty because that's how they learn and develop – we'll take care of getting their clothes clean.' Unilever called this brand positioning 'Dirt is Good' and when it was first introduced under the OMO brand name in Turkey and Brazil in 2003 it was a big hit. These brands acquired great resonance by focusing on the subject with most relevance for mums – their children's development. So simple and powerful was the Dirt is Good message that when tested amongst mums it prompted a cathartic release, many had tears in their eyes.

In 2005, Aline Santos, the Global SVP for Unilever's Dirt is Good brand, took up the charge. As Santos spread the radical new positioning around the globe so sales have similarly increased. Brand revenue is up from €330m when Arkwright started to champion the cause to €3.2bn in 2010 when Santos completed the global rollout: 'Success has a very sweet taste', she says.

This is more than just a new communication idea; it has unlocked broader opportunities for innovation. Just as the Dirt is Good message has struck a profound chord with mums all over the world (in Turkey 500,000 of them are Omo's Facebook friends), so has it galvanised the brand team. This clever and simple 'central organising thought' has enabled Unilever people spread across many different countries to get behind a single north star. Now technical development is focused on the kind of stains that kids get (think grass stains not wine stains). Promotional activity is focused around the big idea of allowing kids getting dirty and learning. The brand attracts the best talent in the company and partner agencies around the world.

The story of Dirt is Good is all the more interesting given the internal resistance towards it initially. Unilever has a proud history of getting things clean which in many parts of the world isn't just an aesthetic benefit – clean hands, clean skin, clean dishes, these are not trivial issues. Embracing the Dirt is Good positioning was a big deal for Unilever. After 100 years saying 'Dirt is Bad' to change to 'Dirt is Good' was challenging. Santos says that 'the main problem was not the consumers but the internal resistance to change, we had to convince each of the countries about the power of the idea, country by country, region by region, but with passion we got there.' Whereas Unilever's detergent brands were a mix of different messages, today Dirt is Good has unified several brands globally and is widely recognised as a brilliant and brave move.

> ❝
>
> *The main thing is to keep the main thing the main thing*
>
> Variously attributed

There is an intriguing dilemma in creating 'headspace' for innovators. Do you get the knife out and cut initiatives (something Steve Jobs did successfully when he returned to Apple in 1997 and halted hundreds of projects), or do you replace confusion with inspiration and clarity? To me the Dirt is Good story is a great example of how, when a diverse team gets an inspirational level of focus, it's a lot easier to say 'No' to wayward initiatives and concentrate on the main thing.

Safe Zones

To launch the Features Store, an online or in-branch tool that allows you to customise almost every aspect of your banking relationship, Barclays pulled together a team of 50 experts, drawn from every part of the bank. They were located together and given 90 days to integrate over 2000 separate operations into one smooth offer. Steve Cooper, Barclays UK Retail and Business Bank Chief Products & Segments Officer, comments that 'All the right people could talk to each other rather than email and they were all in it together – from the very start of the project all the way to launch, the sense of excitement and responsibility was palpable. This is a new way of working and has knock-on benefits as each member of the team will eventually spill it out elsewhere in the bank'. Cooper adds that the original estimate was 18 months to crack the challenge, the reason it was achieved in 3 months was the co-location and separation from the mothership.

Innovators need protecting from the corporate machine. They need safe zones where they are insulated from conventional wisdom and can think and experiment freely. This can be achieved by physically separating an innovation team from the mothership or carving out part of an employee's working week to be focused on innovation. There are some clear watch-outs in creating these safe zones. They need a greater degree of continuity than the wider organisation is used to, genuine independence, endorsement from the top, a 'lightning rod' structure to resolve issues fast and an investment in new skills.

66

Innovation always has been driven by a person or a small team that has the luxury of thinking of a new idea and pursuing it. There are no counter examples. It was true 100 years ago and it'll be true for the next 100 years.

Eric Schmidt, former Google CEO, in an interview with
McKinsey Quarterly (2008)

Innovation safe zones must be staffed by people prepared to stick with the innovation all the way to launch. This continuity breeds a great deal of responsibility. A good example of this is LoveFilm, one of Europe's fastest growing businesses. LoveFilm started life in 2002 posting DVDs to homes. After watching a movie you would post it back, soon to receive another DVD from your favourites list. Simon Calver, CEO from 2006 to 2012, led a period of rapid growth and transformed the business into a powerful digital entertainment organisation. Whilst Blockbuster struggled with shops, Calver has driven LoveFilm online and instant. The business was acquired by Amazon in 2012.

66

Innovation needs a small number of the right people, no more than a pizza will feed

Disruptive innovation like this is by definition a shock to the system and needs a different kind of organisational architecture. Small groups of people need to be able to work at pace and unfettered by the activities of the original business. So rather than squeeze innovation into the existing company structure, Calver shaped the business to fit innovation. For many executives, out went job roles and in came innovation projects. Borrowing a leaf from Amazon's book, key executives were organised into 'Pizza Teams'. Calver says: 'Innovation needs a small number of the right people, no more than a pizza will feed, then they must stick with the project – fast tracking it all the way through to launch, they can cut through, there's no baton dropping and lots of pride in ownership'.

Safe zones need the licence to get on and do things differently. Samsung Electronics has several agile Product Innovation Teams (PITs) spread around the world that work along highly entrepreneurial lines. The head of each PIT has a close relationship with HQ in South Korea but also considerable freedom to recruit the best local talent and pursue projects. Samsung back only a limited number of innovation projects each year, this breeds a healthy level of competition internally amongst the PITs. Only experienced innovators and strong decision makers can thrive in this culture. Unlike Samsung, many organisations overly 'parent' their innovation teams. In my view it's far healthier to recruit the right leader (the 'Captain One Minute, Pirate the Next') and let them get on with it.

A version of the internal innovation team is an 'Incubation Team'. This is a small group or people, some of whom are recruited from outside the organisation. Their job is to scour technologies and interesting ideas that exist inside and outside the organisation. The skills of this team are around external collaboration and acquisition. The idea is to forge a relationship with an external party, incubate new businesses to a point where the mothership has extracted useful information or integrates the new company. Incubators need an experienced executive to hold together a diverse team. They need to be credible with entrepreneurs, investors and the most senior leaders within their company.

Safe zones don't mean abandoned zones. If innovation seems to slow down and get stuck, the innovation team needs to know there is a practical way to move things forward.

The most practical way of dealing with the treacle (or the molasses) was told to me by Dr Curtis Carlson, President and CEO of SRI International and a member of President Obama's National Advisory Council on Innovation and Entrepreneurship. SRI was founded in 1946 as Stanford Research Institute. SRI formally separated from the University in 1970 and changed its name to SRI International in 1977. Currently, SRI's R&D labs in Silicon Valley, California, and facilities throughout the United States create new technologies, some of which are spun off into new companies. SRI invented the computer mouse, HD TV and, more recently, Siri, the virtual personal assistant acquired by Apple and installed in the iPhone 4s. Carlson told me of a bypass structure at SRI called the 'Watering Hole'.

The idea is that a project can't always wait for the next scheduled meeting. Sometimes the project champions need help and they need it fast. So a Watering Hole is a 'value-creation forum' that a wide variety of people attend, often Carlson himself. This is an opportunity to change course and improve quickly, with everyone focused on the best outcome for the opportunity, client, or marketplace. Branding the meeting 'The Watering Hole' is very clever. It's clear it's a special meeting where all the animals of the jungle (that is, different points of view within an organisation) come together to work on the same project. It's refreshing and you want to stay focused on the task at hand!

The skills executives need in their innovation safe zones are different to those needed elsewhere in the organisation. Many companies recruit enthusiastic managers and train them as creative 'ninja level' facilitators – skilled innovation champions, ready to spring into action throughout an organisation. With practice these creative ninjas can get very good at running 'expansive' meetings, designing a quest for provocation and experimental 'make it real' processes. People with these skills are invaluable in large businesses and the idea is that as they infect others with their skill and enthusiasm the innovative capability of an organisation gradually increases. These innovation 'muscle build' regimes are easy to sign up to but sustaining them requires a serious commitment to recruiting the right candidates. It's all too tempting to train up highly enthusiastic people, but if they don't have gravitas or the respect of their colleagues then the programme rapidly backfires and it will be several years before the 'innovation' word reappears.

Leadership Models

Rarely are agile teams or safe zones enough to drive innovation through a large organisation. Innovation has to be led from the top. The most extreme examples of 'leader-led' innovation are fashion houses where the leaders have – or surround themselves with people with – great taste. The leader, through some combination of foresight, reputation and charisma, is capable of not just reflecting customer needs but creating them.

The most famous example of strong innovation leadership must be Steve Jobs' leadership of Apple. My take-out from the visits I've made to the Apple headquarters at 1 Infinite Loop has been that it feels more like a fashion house than any other type of business. The folk at Apple have a clear philosophy that creates fashion. There appears to be little need to listen to consumers, which can seem like arrogance; but why listen when you're so clear about the way things should be? Apple has a hyperactive and adoring fan base and, of course, an obsession with sensual detail. It's 'fashion making' leadership like this that makes work tremendously exciting and creates a deep well of loyalty and hard work.

Much of our work in ?What If!'s Shanghai office involves partnering Western companies adapting to the local market. We studied the success of KFC in China, part of the Yum! Group (which also owns Pizza Hut and Taco Bell). It's one of the most successful Western companies in China and certainly the most successful Western quick service restaurant in China.

Last time I was in a KFC in China, I recognised some items on the menu, but only some. Colonel Sanders' famous fried chicken was there, but also an array of items local to Chinese tastes: Youtiao (deep fried breadsticks), congee (traditional porridge) and egg tarts.

Jing-Shyh 'Sam' Su, Vice Chairman of the global Yum! group and CEO of Yum! China Division, led KFC's explosive growth in China in the early 1990s, when there were less than five restaurants. Today there are close to 4000 restaurants, and they have added more than 500 stores in 2011. While KFC growth has stalled in the US, it's shooting ahead in China. KFC China's revenue has overtaken the US, and become a significant profit contributor to Yum's global business. Sam Su, originally from Taiwan and a graduate of Wharton and Procter and Gamble, is a single powerful leader who has led the team to foster outstanding innovation.

Starting in the early 1990s, Sam Su has built a team that has an understanding of Chinese culture. Determined that KFC should not be seen as an American invasion, he reframed the challenge as creating a fast food restaurant chain that would best serve the local Chinese consumer. He set about understanding Chinese consumer insights, researching and developing local menus. In China, KFC will introduce maybe 20 to 30 new menu items a year whereas in the rest of the world this number is in single figures.

Food is an important part of life in China where palates have thousands of years of history behind them. KFC has approached this sensitively with a brand that has inspiring foreign appeal with strong local meaning and commitment, all backed with flawless execution.

KFC's growth story would not have happened if the China team had rigidly followed the western model. A senior executive for Yum! China comments that Sam Su's ability to create a China insight-focused company culture has been critical: 'You can't have a strong ego here, it is all about teamwork'. She adds that Sam Su's leadership encourages breakthrough thinking and endless know-how building.

To other multinational companies, stepping back to allow for localisation is no small decision. Only leaders can decide how to tinker with a business model like this. In KFC's case it's worked very successfully.

Some organisations are so large and so diverse that they need more distributed forms of innovation leadership. Increasingly companies are appointing a Chief Innovation Officer. This is a relatively new role. The idea is that an experienced innovator will be able to focus 100% on innovation and make connections between silos.

A CIO may have several subteams reporting in to them: innovation projects teams, an incubator unit and maybe an open innovation team.

A CIO needs to be an experienced and tough character. They need to influence and spread best practice without the power base that comes with a revenue stream. So they need an excellent 'sponsor' relationship with the CEO as well as terrific networking and influencing skills.

The most effective CIOs I have met talk a lot about what everyone else is achieving. They are extremely generous in their praise.

The Grapevine

What if I told you there was an office-based communication system that had the following features:

- extremely fast operating speed

- instant updates

- unlimited RAM

- constant peer review

- showcases what everyone is doing

- specialises in exposing hypocrisy

- inextinguishable

- completely free!

What if I told you that?

It's called 'The Grapevine' – the informal transmission of data or rumour from person to person at work. This gossip-fuelled system is one of the most powerful elements of the corporate apparatus. Just because it's underground and unregulated doesn't mean we shouldn't take it seriously. People won't admit it openly, but the fact is they often don't expect innovation to go anywhere. They've seen it happen before and word on the street is that if you take a risk, you get your knuckles rapped, so better just to keep one's head down and wait until it's all blown over. The Grapevine is a powerful force – we need it to work for innovation, and not against it.

Pssst – have you heard this?

> 'Hey, keep this under your hat but I just heard that Fatima got bawled out by the boss. He said he wanted brave ideas so she took him one – and look what happened. Keep your heads down.'

> 'Hey, I heard that Nicki's been talking to a competitor about a JV. I thought her boss would have killed her but apparently he likes the audacity of the idea!'

> 'Hey, I heard they're thinking of giving Dave a shot at the Marketing Director job. Apparently he's been holding brand development meetings in customer's homes, kind of makes them feel closer to the market.'

Buried in all of these corridor conversations are serious messages about the competence of individuals, their leaders and the organisation as a whole. Sift out the salacious elements of gossip and you'll find important commentary that sets expectations about how we should behave at work. The Grapevine is the unofficial but authoritative guidebook to what's OK and not OK.

The Grapevine takes what has happened in the past and moulds it as a kind of advertising campaign for what you can expect to happen in the future. This is important because innovation needs people at all levels in an organisation to be able to share their unformed thoughts, and it needs leaders to listen hard and help grow the idea or gently reject it. So the reputation of key people is critical. Are they good listeners? Is it OK to approach the boss and share an idea? Will they bawl me out? Will they fob me off? Will they be interested in what I have to say? It's how these questions have been answered for others that gets amplified over the Grapevine.

How does the Grapevine work?

The exposé

It's delightfully rewarding to spot where someone says one thing but does another. So the Grapevine is very good at exposing hypocrisy, attacking the braggart and sympathising with the underdog.

A dose of shock and awe

Like advertising, content on the grapevine won't cut through unless there's as element of excitement or the thrill associated with knowing something slightly shocking.

Tiny details make big stories

Like a bird of prey, always scanning, ready to pounce on the slightest detail – the Grapevine means you need to be super accurate with your words. No place more so than the issue of top team alignment. The slightest hint of a chink of light between the senior team will get picked over on the Grapevine.

The Grapevine just grows stronger if you try to control it. Ask anyone who has lived under a harsh political regime. The more the official line is distrusted the more currency the Grapevine acquires. But there is one way the Grapevine can be deliberately exploited in order to innovate better.

This is where 'storytelling' comes in. Stories are the oldest currency of news and the Grapevine loves them. Have you ever told a story only to hear it boomerang back to you years later? You've been forgotten as the teller, but the story lives on as a sort of corporate legend.

So what does a good story look like? Within each story there is always a core of five elements – can you spot each element in the story I'm about to tell you?

This is a story about practising what you preach.

I was once in the middle of a tough innovation assignment. The client was a major global bank and we were working on new models of service excellence. My contact, the head of the retail bank, was a real tough cookie. Every time we met he grilled me, he pushed at each idea and he really stretched me. Although this kind of challenge is useful we didn't have a great relationship. I was looking forward to the all day offsite meeting about as much as I look forward to a trip to the dentist.

The offsite was on a Monday. I remember it because this ruined my weekend. So when the day itself arrived I steeled myself to go into work, trying not to think 'I can't wait for six o'clock'. But something odd happened. From the minute I walked into the room the client was different. He strode up, greeted me warmly and introduced me to his team. And you know what – we had a great day. In just a few hours we nailed down some outstanding new ideas around better service in the bank. The icing on the cake came at the end of the day when he announced that phase two of the work was mine!

The next day I found out what had happened. One of my team, Robyn, had gone to Heathrow Airport on the Sunday afternoon to personally welcome the clients who had flown in from all over Europe. Robyn figured that as our project was about great service then she should demonstrate this to the inbound bank executives. She knew that traveling on a Sunday is ruinous for family life and that the client would really appreciate a friendly welcome, a ticket for the superfast train into London Paddington and a reservation for the whole team that evening at a local restaurant. She had even visited the hotel to check the arrangements, leaving instructions in the rooms on how to get to our offices together with a suggestion of a couple of bars to visit after the restaurant. Maybe not surprisingly our clients had a great evening. They soon forgot how unpleasant it is to travel on a Sunday and had a terrific evening out. Over dinner they discussed the great service they'd had from Robyn and how it had such an impact on them, they resolved to drive their service project harder.

To me this really shows the power of practising what you preach.

OK – enjoy the story? Did you get all the five points? Give yourself a star for each.

Star 1: Why am I going to tell you this story?

Upfront I told you that this was a story about practising what you preach.

Star 2: Who is the hero?

This can never be the storyteller. That would make it a 'boast' and not a story. In this case it was Robyn.

Star 3: Where's the drama?

A good story has a pattern. Things look bleak. Then the hero saves the day – just in the nick of time. In this case I wasn't looking forward to the meeting, but out of nowhere, and most surprisingly, it turned out great.

Star 4: What's the payoff?

In this case, getting phase two was a huge payoff. I didn't say it in the story but Robyn was also appreciated for doing her job well.

Star 5: Why have I just told you this story?

I repeat the point of the story in my last line.

Telling a 'five star' story is very effective. People 'get' it and remember it. As a technique it is easy to learn, remember and self-moderate.

So what's the narrative you want in your organisation around innovation strategy and innovation behaviours? Use any opportunity you can to tell the stories you want to be circulating. At team meetings, off-sites, in the lunch queue, the company newsletter, standing at the urinal, on posters in reception, in your weekly update emails to staff – these are all great opportunities to insert your stories. If they're good enough they might get re-told.

Don't expect the good stuff that's happening to spread by osmosis. Get out there and tell people about it, and then tell it again, and again… Many years ago, on a ?What If! TopDog study tour of the US, we visited the Rochester New York-based grocery chain Wegmans. They told me something I'd never forget. They said if you wanted to really land a message, you had to repeat it. Their rule of thumb was to repeat key messages seven times. That didn't mean they literally repeated the message seven times but that they ensured that over time important messages to shoppers and colleagues were repeated in many different formats, and at least seven times. I was struck by how poor the much-too-polite Brits are at this and how good the Americans are. The funny thing was that during the week, we visited some terrific businesses and now, maybe ten years later, I can still only remember the message from Wegmans.

But the most effective way to create stories with real viral horsepower is to get noticed for what you actually do. I used to work in Thailand and I had a boss who lived in Australia. When he visited he would land at the airport, go to his hotel and freshen up. But he wouldn't come into the office. He'd be out in what we used to call the 'field' – this meant he hung out with normal people in normal homes doing normal stuff. The next day when he did come into the office he was very informed about who bought our products and why. He didn't talk much about strategy or research but was able to relate everything we were trying to do to the reality of the marketplace. The story of 'The Boss That Didn't Come Into The Office' became legend and really set the narrative for the rest of us. There was no doubt that getting close to customers was our job.

What is instructive about this and many other resilient Grapevine stories is that it was based on an observation of what someone actually did, not what they said others should do. I think the lesson for innovators is that you have to be the change you want to see in others. If you need more customer connection at work, then start off by connecting yourself. This will get noticed and before long – if you are authentic in your actions – it will become a story on the Grapevine that others will emulate.

66

Nothing travels faster than the speed of light,
with the possible exception of bad news,
which obeys its own special laws

Douglas Adams. *Mostly Harmless.* Pan Books, UK (1992)

Making Metrics Meaningful

Like all commercial activities, innovation needs performance metrics. But innovation isn't like all commercial activities, it carries significantly more risk (and reward) than something that's been done many times before.

66

For the most part, normal accounting doesn't work for innovation

NPV calculations to assess the return on investment for a late stage project, or the value of a portfolio or pipeline of late stage projects are useful. But for the most part, normal accounting doesn't work for innovation. Early stage initiatives that get burdened with making an overly precise financial case create artificial results and demoralise the innovation team. In the end no one wins.

I have found that stage gate processes often force unrealistic quantitative forecasts on innovation initiatives too early in the process. This creates a couple of problems. First, innovation modelling is subject to gaming; a 1% increase in our revenue assumptions compounds to make a huge difference to revenues ten years later. But the commercial world does not have a good track record estimating the scale of innovation: Viagra, Facebook, Google, iTunes – all huge innovations, yet none of their of growth was predicted. Second, there's a double uncertainty to measuring 'over the horizon' innovation. Discounted cash analysis often paints an optimistic picture as it measures an uncertain upside versus steady state finances – but as we all know, if we don't innovate our state will be anything but steady; at best uncertain, but probably declining. Conventional accounting isn't built to handle this much uncertainty.

Innovators need to propose how they will be measured very early on. If they don't, they'll find the CFO has imposed measures on them.

Early stage innovation needs people to talk frequently about the development of the idea. So it makes sense to design measures that promote dialogue and engage stakeholders. Too few ideas in the pipeline – let's talk about that. Too many ideas – well let's talk about that too. Just the right number of ideas in the pipeline – hmmm, that's too good to be true, now we really need to talk.

I have found that it is simple metrics like the following that promote the right sort of dialogue around innovation:

1. **Look top-down at the innovation pipeline** on an order of magnitude basis. Contrast the non-risk adjusted pipeline value with the innovation target (the growth gap). If the pipeline value is ten times the target, then maybe that's good enough – very simple, very fast and very likely to provoke a debate.

2. **Do a straightforward risk-adjusted valuation** of individual initiatives and ladder up to the total risk-adjusted pipeline. If that doesn't hit the desired financial outcome from innovation then how many more probes and projects do we need today? In other words, are we kissing enough frogs? Working this through with a client recently we were able to show that they probably needed three more projects to hit their objectives – unwelcome but important news.

3. **Analyse the speed and success rate** of initiatives flowing through the stage gate process. How quickly are we prototyping ideas, moving them on or rejecting them? Effectively you are measuring idea 'flow speed' (or conversely pipeline 'stickiness'). Like unsold inventory, there's a cost to stalled ideas.

4. **Dig underneath the financial value** of an idea for the underlying value drivers. So instead of spending time measuring, say, the value of a solar panel innovation project, track the drivers of solar panel growth: new home construction, changes in technology efficiency or government legislation. Measuring changes in value drivers will provoke a lively discussion with the sponsor team.

5. **Establish a market valuation model** that allows innovators to put their money where their mouth is. The value of each innovation initiative is then decided by a venture board composed of a few wise heads and external advisors. The Incubator team members can buy options – but real cash must change hands. In a similar way

the Financial Services sector likes predictive markets – trading ideas using a virtual currency. GE pushes many of its initiatives to joint venture, calculating this will 'prove them out' better than actuarial techniques.

6. **Monitor incubator health metrics.** How engaged are the team? What is their reputation? What's the ratio of the team's 'useful time' to 'form filling, courses and reporting'? How many unsolicited job applications? For example, Boeing tracks 'how often the incubator asks for help' as a useful and telling measure.

Finally there is another way to look at making a business case for innovation. Let me call it the 'Free Bet'. Think of it as an innovation measure that gives comfort about the downside rather than raising expectation about the upside.

The Free Bet does not promise what revenue, profits or market share you are going to achieve. This upside accounting just shines a light on innovation – if the rewards are this big now, everyone wants to know what's going on. Also it's highly unlikely your upside estimates are going to be correct, something your boss knows very well.

Antony Jenkins, CEO at Barclays Retail and Business bank, eschews conventional investment metrics when it comes to innovation. You might think that such an august institution would have measured the hell out of everything but Jenkins believes that 'when it comes to early stage innovation, NPV calculations, models and spreadsheets have too many assumptions to be useful'. When the Oyster credit card was developed, Jenkins had not asked 'How much money will we make?' but 'How much do we need to spend to find out if this works?'. He adds 'on this basis we just took a decision, we didn't want to analyse this to death.'

> *Far better to pin your colours to a minimal downside number than an aggressive upside number*

So with innovation you are sometimes better off using this 'downside' accounting. Work out how much it costs to get to the next significant stage of the project – maybe to get to the end of a pilot project or to a soft launch. If the boss knows you're not placing a mega bet, that the worst case isn't that bad, then they're much more likely to agree to it. Far better to pin your colours to a minimal downside number than an aggressive upside number.

Downside accounting enables an entrepreneurial approach – undercover and lean activity. You're going to break even or lose no more than a certain amount. So now there is a green light and you can get on and do what you have to do to get the initiative to the next stage of development.

Winning Over the Naysayers

In a large company the reality is an idea will have many hands on it. There are many opportunities for it to be touched and slightly altered along its journey. Each change may seem insignificant but in total the once great idea can easily be compromised to death.

So it's important that we anticipate all the issues that may crop up. In addition, it's likely that some stakeholders will be glass-half-empty characters. We need them to unfold their arms and open up to possibilities.

There are two practical activities that will melt the hardest critic into a purring pussycat. First, get business leaders face to face with their consumers. This is an incredibly valuable exercise. Although it sounds an obvious idea, it is surprising how little this happens, especially with executives in operations, finance, IT and other roles that don't consider themselves 'customer facing'. Direct interaction builds their confidence when they're making a 'Go/No go' decision. They're analysing the numbers, but they're remembering the customers they met. In my experience, seeing the whites of the consumers' eyes has an amazing power to transform a sceptic into an advocate.

Second, build pockets of optimism. Everyone wants to be connected with a successful innovation and everyone loves telling and retelling stories about how something audacious and unusual has worked out brilliantly. Our experience is that naysayers can't argue with success. So quickly create a small success. Be clear about why this project was a success. Maybe it was the way you framed the challenge, the quest for provocation that you went on or the way you made ideas real. If you can clearly point to the contributors of success then even the most critical naysayer will struggle to say why you shouldn't repeat them. Essentially you are trying to give innovation a good name. You are championing a new way. This means you have to go out of your way to demonstrate why innovation has worked and that the rewards have been worth it.

Top naysayisms

1. *'Experimentation, prototyping, beta testing – sure, great for tech start-ups but this is a pharmaceutical company – we can't just meddle around with customers or physicians like that! There are rules.'*

It's true that some industries like the airplane industry, banking or healthcare are steeped in regulation, high capital costs and long development cycles. Here the quick turnaround regime of experimentation seems beyond reach. But don't give up; the danger is of course that these organisations don't try anything new and become numb to genuine entrepreneurial activity. Scour the cupboards for what you can change in the short term. If you can't change the molecules, can you change the packaging?

2. *'We're an engineering based organisation, we have 99% rational criti-cal thinkers, we don't do ambiguity and we don't sit around on bean bags brainstorming all day.'*

True, brainstorming – particularly with a large group – can be unwieldy and produce a series of shallow ideas leaving everyone dis-satisfied. Or, a brainstorm that is skilfully and sensitively managed can move a team on a long way. There should be no controversy over a brainstorm – a bad one is a waste of time and a good one is invaluable.

Actually engineers make good iterators – they quickly get the princi-ples behind experimentation. The argument is that a series of mini experiments means that it never feels too late or too career damag-ing to pull out of the experiment altogether. The history of innov-ation is littered with stories of organisations that have become too wedded to things and as a result have stopped seeing things clearly. So, far from being flaky, a programme of 'planned ambiguity' actu-ally reduces risk.

Let's Get Practical

There is an undeniable truth to innovating in a large organisation: change, especially disruptive change, will always meet resistance. This is just how it is. My observation is that a lot of time spent complaining about this 'truth' could be better spent facing up to the reality of the situation and making a plan to combat it. In other words, if you find yourself bruised from battling the corporate machine, then just get over it. All your battles can be anticipated and to an extent, pre-empted.

So before you start to innovate, when the word is just a twinkle in your eye, gather your team, away from the office and over the course of a day make a battle plan. Don't leave the room until you have clear answers to the following:

* Have you framed the innovation challenge? How much, what type and by when?

* Are you clear what is in scope and what is out of scope?

* How will you use the grapevine to manage your reputation?

* How will you demonstrate love for your products over love for the process?

* What's the single, simple north star that will create headspace to innovate?

* Where are the safe zones that will protect young ideas?

* What role does the company leader need to play?

* How are you going to recommend to your sponsor group that they measure you?

* Who are the naysayers? What's the plan to get them on-side?

A Call to Arms

I hope this book has made you think again and that you're excited by the challenge ahead of you. There isn't much more rewarding in life than staring at a blank page and then filling it with something of value – something you can point at and say 'I did that!' I hope this book has given you some ideas about what you can do to accelerate the innovation journey and shown you that there is indeed a science to serendipity.

Clearly the context for this book has not been entrepreneurial start-ups. Organisations at that heady stage of development don't need business books. Instead the common theme stranded through this book is the potentially corrosive impact a large organisation can have on our ability to innovate. This, to my mind, is a natural evolutionary fact of commercial life. But I do want to correct any misconceptions. I'm not saying that big is bad. In fact, get the corporate machine behind you and innovation can be a huge force for good in the world. It is simply my belief that we now know enough about how innovation works in large organisations to pre-empt the inevitable roadblocks. I don't think this was true 20 or even 10 years ago.

In this book I've switched between the words 'serendipity' and 'innovation'. I see them as very similar concepts. Serendipity is the clever connection between seemingly unconnected points. The kind of thing people look at and say 'That's so clever and so simple – why didn't I think of that?' But serendipity is more than that; it's the useful application of these connections – there has to be some sort of benefit or impact. Innovation is the creation of new value – the meaning is very similar.

To me serendipity is a fascinating concept because it unlocks how the innovator's journey feels from the inside. You set out, determined to make a change. You realise you need to 'unlearn' all that's got you into a rut. You immerse yourself in a world of provocative stimulus. Without over-thinking the challenge, you experiment with the ideas that present themselves to you. Clever experimentation engages the corporate machine and, before you know it, there's a head of steam behind your idea and a launch date pencilled in the diary.

What might look like a lucky series of coincidences to an outsider is really the result of a lot of hard work. Only you know how much the quest for provocation has cost you, or how many of the experiments didn't pay off. And only you know how much time you spent engaging your stakeholders. Your lips are sore with all those frogs you've kissed – only you know that. That's why I like this term serendipity. To an outsider, it's magic. To an insider, it's hard graft – something you just feel compelled to do.

So, good luck. But by now you know that this is just a romantic figure of speech. I wish you all the best, but the luck you make yourself.

Thanks

Thanks to the many clients of ?What If! and other respected business leaders who have helped make my stories come alive and this book feel, I hope, so practical.

Thanks to the many ?What If!ers who helped me write this book – either through the many examples of your courage to try yet more new things, or your unflagging support and helpful comments. Thanks particularly to Barrie Berg, for such wise counsel, Andy Comer for the many edits and re-edits, Kirsty Johnson for designing her first book, Ben Stevens for managing some great photos, Alison Bowditch for pulling no punches, Sal Pajwani for many great ideas, Robin Price for ensuring I didn't bankrupt the company, Leanne Gilbert for managing my time, Sarah Smith for her diligent research and Sarah Peachey for her eagle eye. Thanks also to the many ?What If!ers who allowed themselves to be photographed while at work.

Thanks to Holly Bennion and Jenny Ng at Wiley for keeping me on track.

Thanks to Jake Hilder of www.jakehilderphotography.co.uk for many of the photos.

Last but not least a huge thank you to my wonderful kids, Holly and Harry, and my wife Alice who never once mentioned how sunny it was outside or that just maybe I should take a break. Thanks for leaving me alone; without your support, belief and endless cups of tea I wouldn't have got past Chapter 1.

Sources

Introduction: The Real Heroes of Innovation

♦ The Viagra story is based on interviews with Dr David Brown. For more detail see his lecture at the Centre for Entrepreneurial Learning, The Judge Business School, University of Cambridge. http://www.cfel.jbs.cam.ac.uk/programmes/enterprisetuesday/videos.html

♦ The Julius Comroe quote is from *Retrospectroscope: Insights into Medical Discovery* by Julius H. Comroe. Von Gehr Publisher, 1977.

♦ If you're interested in the role luck plays in business try *Great by Choice: Uncertainty, Chaos, and Luck – Why Some Thrive Despite Them All*, by Jim Collins and Morten T. Hansen. 2011. Harper Collins. Another excellent book on the subject is *Get Lucky: How to Put Planned Serendipity to Work for You and Your Business* by Thor Muller and Lane Becker. Jossey Bass. 2012.

Chapter 1 The Protagonist

♦ The Axe/Lynx story is based on interviews with Unilever executives and Neil Munn who was Axe/Lynx brand director between 2002 and 2006.

♦ Victoria Beckham's quote from *Learning to Fly: The Autobiography*. Penguin Global, 2005.

♦ For more on emotionally compelling and stretching goals there is still no better than *Built to Last* by James Collins and Jerry Porras. Random House Business Books. 2005. BHAGs (Big Hairy Audacious Goals) must be one of the best business terms ever coined.

♦ The ASOS and the Harvard Bioscience stories are based on interviews with senior executives.

* The final quote from Nick Robertson is taken from 'An Interview with Nick Robertson – CEO of ASOS' by Medhi Jaffer and Tom Bordell. Varsity.co.uk, 14 October 2011. http://www.varsity.co.uk/news/3845

* Photo of David Green holding the trachea by Deborah Becker Mclennan.

* For an excellent discussion of the pirate mentality, read *The Pirate Inside* by Adam Morgan. John Wiley & Sons, Ltd, 2004.

* Readers familiar with Maurice Belbin's work on team roles will recognise the 'completer finisher'. I have always understood this to be an almost obsessive need for accuracy. This is different from the finishing skills innovators need. My view of a good 'finisher' is someone with the tenacity and responsibility to complete the task, without getting distracted by other exciting challenges.

Chapter 2 The Quest for Provocation

* The stories about the global insurance company, the bakery executives visiting their customers at breakfast, the confectionary executives and the Consumer Shoes exercise, the psoriasis suffers and the 'Future of Sex' projects are based on ?What If! work with our client partners.

* Steve Jobs quote from 'The Next Insanely Great Thing' by Gary Wolf. *Wired*, 1996.

* The Kodak story is well known and the comments are from *Changing Focus: Kodak and the Battle to Save a Great American Company* by Alecia Swasy. Times Business, Random House, 1997.

* The Encyclopaedia Britannica story comes from interviews with senior executives who have since left the business.

* Fresh & Easy quotes are from *The Economist*, 21 June 2007 and William Kay, 'Tesco Admits: We got it Wrong in US', *The Sunday Times*, 22 February 2009.

- The Bullet Train story is found at 'Innovation inspired by nature Biomimicry' by K.D. Hargroves, M.H. Smith. *Ecos* (129), 27–28 (2006).

- The easyJet and BP Invigorate story are based on ?What If! projects.

- Photo of the screen obsessed driver – I took this early one morning on my iPhone.

- The quote by Paul Flory is found in *Serendipity, Accidental Discoveries in Science* by Royston M. Roberts. John Wiley & Sons, Ltd, 1989.

Chapter 3 Making Ideas Real

- Stories and references to Boots, 48 (Telefonica), Dyson, Metro, Barclays, Google and SRI are based on interviews with senior executives.

- The Dyson story is supplemented by quotes from *Against the Odds: An Autobiography* by James Dyson. Orion Publishing, 1997.

- Photos of Dave teaching me the offside trap by Jake Hilder.

- The Edison quotes:

  'If I find 10,000 ways something won't work, I haven't failed. I am not discouraged, because every wrong attempt discarded is often a step forward ...' http://www.thomasedison.com/quotes.html

  'I never did anything worth doing entirely by accident ... Almost none of my inventions were derived in that manner. They were achieved by having trained myself to be analytical and to endure and tolerate hard work.' http://www.thomasedison.com/quotes.html

  'Show me a thoroughly satisfied man and I will show you a failure.' *The Diary and Sundry Observations of Thomas Alva Edison* (1948), p. 110. wikiquote.org/wiki/Thomas Edison

'Just because something doesn't do what you planned it to do doesn't mean it's useless.' http://www.quotationspage.com/quote/394.html

'Restlessness is discontent, and discontent is the first necessity of progress.' http://quotationsbook.com/quote/32668/

'Genius is 1% inspiration and 99% perspiration. Accordingly, a "genius" is often a talented person who has done his or her homework.' http://www.thomasedison.com/quotes.html

+ The egg drop experiment is fascinating – read more at 'Efficacy of Prototyping Under Time Constraints' by Steven P. Dow, Kate Heddleston, Scott R. Klemmer. Stanford University HCI Group. Department of Computer Science, 26–30 October 2009.

+ The birth of Gü was told to me by founder James Averdieck.

+ Jeff Bezos quote from 'Blind-Alley Explorer', *Businessweek*, 19 August 2004. http://www.businessweek.com/bwdaily/dnflash/aug2004/nf20040819_7348_db_81.htm

+ The Frappuccino story is found in *Pour Your Heart into It. How Starbucks Built a Company One Cup at a Time* by Howard Schultz and Dori Jones Yang. Hyperion, 1999.

Chapter 4 Collision Course

+ The Method, Google, Innocent stories were researched during visits between 2009 and 2012 and discussion with senior executives.

+ All photos by Jake Hilder except the Method pictures which I took on my iPhone, the TV and European retailer shots taken by ?!ers and the Zappos photos supplied by Zappos. Many thanks to UKTV, Google and Zappos for their help.

- The speech by Winston Churchill to the English Architecture Association was reported in 1924.

- To read more on Brad Bird's story go to 'Innovation Lessons from Pixar: An Interview with Oscar-winning Director Brad Bird' by Hayagreeva Rao, Robert Sutton and Allen P. Webb. *McKinsey Quarterly*, April 2008. http://www.mckinseyquarterly.com/Innovation_lessons_from_Pixar_ An_interview_with_Oscar-winning_director_Brad_Bird_2127_abstract

- For more on cubicles and the apology look at Julie Schlosser, 'Cubicles: The Great Mistake'. *Fortune Magazine* 2006. http://money.cnn. com/2006/03/09/magazines/fortune/cubicle_howiwork_fortune/

- For more on the Valve handbook go to valvesoftware.com. Also see this interesting article by Shane Show at *Fast Company* on the Valve handbook at http://www.fastcompany.com/1835546/you-re-hired- now-figure-things-out-with-the-help-of-this-whimsical-handbook

- Definition of 'mingle'. Merriam-Webster.com. http://www.merriam- webster.com (April 2012).

- To find out more about PechaKucha go to pecha-kucha.org and klein- dytham.com

- The Zappos story is from *The Zappos Experience* by Joseph A. Michelli. McGraw-Hill, 2012.

- The engagement in workspace design by the University of Exeter is described in The University of Exeter, 'Designing Your Own Workspace Improves Health, Happiness and Productivity', *ScienceDaily*, 7 September 2010. http://www.sciencedaily.com/releas- es/2010/09/100907104035.htm

- In my view the best book on how our physical environment affects us is *A Pattern Language* by Christopher Alexander, Sara Ishikawa and Murray Silverstein. Oxford University Press, 1977.

Chapter 5 Battling the Corporate Machine

* References and stories from Wegmans, Kingfisher, UKTV, Innocent, KFC China, Samsung, Barclays, GE, LoveFilm, Unilever and SRI have been sourced from discussion with senior executives.

* Wikipedia has an excellent history of the 2CV at http://en.wikipedia.org/wiki/Citro%C3%ABn_2CV

* The classic 'my first car' photo was taken by my Mum.

* The loo that doubles as a hand basin kindly supplied by Kingfisher Group.

* The quote from Eric Schmidt is from James Manyika's article: 'Google's View on the Future of Business: An Interview with CEO Eric Schmidt', *McKinsey Quarterly*, September 2008. http://www.mckinseyquarterly.com/Googles_view_on_the_future_of_business_An_interview_with_CEO_Eric_Schmidt_2229

* For more on Samsung's approach to innovation see Yoon C. Lee, Managing Director of Samsung's Global Product Innovation Team talk to the Center on Global Brand Leadership at Columbia Business School. http://www.youtube.com/watch?v=YRCip1KDR18

* Douglas Adams. *Mostly Harmless*. Pan Books, UK, 1992.

* The reference to Boeing sourced from http://www.innovationmanagement.org/Wiki/index.php?title=R%26D_Management.

* A recent survey by IESE and Capgemini Consulting found that 43% of respondents claim to have a formally accountable innovation executive. This was significantly up from the 33% who claimed so in a previous survey. *Innovation Leadership Study*. Capgemini Consulting and IESE Business School. March 2012. Miller, Klokgieters, Brankovic, Duppen.

Index

About Matt Kingdon

Co-founder, co-chairman, and chief enthusiast at ?What If!

Matt Kingdon started ?What If! with Dave Allan in 1992. Their goal: to partner with clients who were enthused about innovation but stuck on how to make it happen.

?What If! has offices in three continents and partners with organisations across all sectors. In 2004 and 2005 ?WhatIf! won unprecedented, back-to-back first place finishes in the 'UK's Best Small Workplaces' awards run by the Great Place to Work Institute and the *Financial Times*.

Co-author of the best-selling innovation text *Sticky Wisdom*, Matt speaks frequently on the subject. 'I've realised how useful it is to make goals tangible and how important it is to relentlessly engage everyone with the excitement and stretch of the journey,' he says. 'We spend too much time at work for it to be predictable.'

Matt's core belief is that the key challenges facing organisations as they transform from sleepy giants to nimble innovators are more human than strategic. Listening, experimenting and packaging new ideas to survive the inevitable corporate beating – these skills, more so than 'clever' thinking and heavyweight documentation, are what separate innovation winners from innovation also-rans.

Prior to ?What If!, Matt worked with Unilever marketing its brand portfolio, first in the UK and then in Southeast Asia and the Middle East. Matt lives in London with his family. His hobby is having cartilage removed from his knees following marathons he shouldn't have run.